Singing for a
Spirit

Singing for a Spirit

A Portrait of the Dakota Sioux

Vine Deloria, Jr.

CLEAR LIGHT PUBLISHERS
SANTA FE, NEW MEXICO

Copyright © 1999 Vine Deloria, Jr.
Clear Light Publishers
823 Don Diego, Santa Fe, NM 87501
WEB: www.clearlightbooks.com

First Edition
10 9 8 7 6 5 4 3 2 1

Library of Congress Cataloging-in-Publication Data

Deloria, Vine, Jr., 1933–
    Singing for a spirit : a portrait of the Dakota Sioux / Vine
Deloria, Jr.
    p. cm.
ISBN 1-57416-025-7
1. Deloria, Philip Joseph. 2. Deloria, Vine, Jr.
3. Yankton Indians—Kings and rulers—Biography.
4. Yankton Indians—Religion. 5. Yankton Indians—
social life and customs.
I. Title.
E99.Y25D45   1999
978'.004975'0092—dc21
[B]   99-25080
                                                    CIP

Production and typography by Carol O'Shea

Cover design by Carol O'Shea
Cover photographs: Thunder Butte, S.D., landscape © by Philip
J. Deloria and portrait of Saswe by unknown photographer, 1868,
author's collection

Contents

Saswe

Dedication

*To that fearless French boy who went west,
and to Saswe, Tipi Sapa, and my father,
Vine Deloria, Sr., who followed the vision*

Acknowledgments

*I wish to thank my father, Vine Deloria, Sr.; my
Aunt Ella Deloria, who told me most of these stories
endlessly so that I would never forget where we came
from; Ray Demallie, who made corrections in the
Dakota words and grammatical structures; and my
cousin Philip Lane, Sr., who told me more stories of
Tipi Sapa, Wakpala, and the past.*

Eagle Nest Butte, South Dakota. Photo © by Philip J. Deloria.

PART I:
A Vision and a Prophecy

Thunder Butte, South Dakota. Photo © by Philip J. Deloria.

Introduction

In the winter of 1916–1917 a devoted Episcopal church-woman, Miss Sarah Emilia Olden, came from the eastern United States to write a book, *The People of Tipi Sapa*, on my grandfather, Philip Joseph Deloria, who was one of the most prominent Native clergy in that denomination. Philip had been chief of Band Eight of the Yankton Sioux tribe as a very young man. Even though he chose to become an Episcopal priest, his people elected him chief several times, so that he had quite a different standing among both missionaries and Indian political leaders than anyone else.

The book reflected the social and religious atmosphere of the day. It gushed in describing the Great Plains, waxed enthusiastic over the progress of Christianity among the Sioux people, and generally assumed that assimilation was a worthy goal for the Sioux people to pursue. But Philip, in his sixties, did not share all of this optimism. Rather, he wanted to talk about the old days, the customs, beliefs, and practices of his people. It was clear that he was becoming disenchanted with the white man's culture and beliefs. They did not seem to him to be any better than what the Sioux had been doing and believing for thousands of years before their contact with Western civilization. He therefore saw the book as a way to pass along to other people something of the days he had known before the Sioux were confined to reservations.

Miss Olden, as people at Wakpala, South Dakota, called her, was not a great researcher or writer. She might, in fact, have been called a scribe or even a secretary, since she wrote down my grandfather's words almost verbatim, at the same time copying paragraphs from mission reports and newsletters as parts of chapters. Thus it appears that some observations were her own when in fact they were those of various people at St. Elizabeth's School, a reservation boarding school provided by the Episcopal Church to the Indian people on the Standing Rock Reservation.

Our family had copies of the book when I was growing up. I remember my aunt Ella Deloria, my father, and other relatives making a special effort to ensure that I knew the "real" versions of some of the stories printed in the book. Thus, while they felt honored to have this book, they were also quite hurt that Miss Olden had divided the stories into disconnected anecdotes and had not included some details they felt were important. As a child, then, I had access to the more extended versions of these stories as well as information on Saswe, my great-grandfather, who was a very powerful medicine man and the person who directed my grandfather along the path to Christianity and the Episcopal priesthood.

Some of the cultural material in *The People of Tipi Sapa* will be familiar to those who have read other materials on traditional Sioux practices and beliefs, such as the Black Elk materials from the Oglala Sioux. My ancestors were part of the most northern and western bands of the Yanktonais Sioux. Though there are some marked differences, I think the materials in this book illustrate how little the basic stories varied over the whole Sioux Nation.

In the interests of accuracy and to enable scholars to use these materials, I have added material from the oral tradition passed down in my family and set it off in brackets. My older relatives were adamant about telling the stories properly, and I hope these variants will prove useful to readers.

Most disappointing to my relatives was the omission by Miss Olden of the real story of our family. Ella suspected that Miss Olden thought these family stories were fables and could not understand that a "pagan" religious tradition could require an Indian family to become Christians for four generations. Everything my family did in this regard was influenced by the spiritual visions of Saswe, my great-grandfather; this by itself probably made Miss Olden unwilling to tell the story.

The opportunity to tell the whole story and to make the cultural materials more accurate was irresistible. It has been my goal to bring together what Sarah Olden recorded and the teachings of my family elders, in effect to write the book they wished she had written.

Saswe

The story behind *The People of Tipi Sapa* goes back to a time when France had not yet been deprived of its North American colonial empire. According to my father, around the 1750s two orphan boys from a good middle-class family in France, Phillipe and François, were brought to America through the good offices of friends of their parents. The family were Hugenots, and their friends became increasingly worried about the religious persecutions in France and believed the family should begin again in the New World.

When the boys were in their late teens, François decided to make his mark in the West while Phillipe decided to remain in the New England area. Some time ago, when trying to do a family genealogy, I discovered a large number of Delorias in upstate New York, New Hampshire, and Vermont, leading me to believe that Phillipe had continued the family in good fashion and left numerous descendants.

François drifted to Quebec and signed on with a fur-trading expedition that was headed through the Great Lakes country to the area around Lake Winnipeg to trade with the tribes of the Canadian plains. François and another young French boy were hired to take care of the horses and do the loading and unloading while the adults of the party killed game and traded with the tribes they encountered.

One day several horses got loose and the boys were sent to fetch them. They traveled quite a distance from camp before they caught the horses, and it looked as if they would barely be able to return before dark. When they arrived at the camp, they found a bloody sight. All the men had been killed, the goods and furs stolen, and whatever was not taken had been destroyed and rendered useless to anyone else. The boys believed the party had gotten on the wrong side of a band of Assiniboines, and the Indians had evened the score.

They faced a real dilemma. They didn't think they could get back to eastern Canada safely with no weapons or provisions. But they knew that the French had settlements in St. Louis and parts of the Illinois country. Having a vague idea of the geography of the region gained from conversations with the men during the journey out, they decided to head due south with the hope of reaching the Missouri River, making a raft, and floating down to St. Louis.

Being young and inexperienced, they had little to eat except berries and the few edible plants they recognized. Soon reduced to near starvation, the boys wandered through the Dakota country in search of the Missouri River. At the Big Bend of the Missouri, south of present-day Pierre, South Dakota, their luck ran out. The other boy died of starvation and illness, and our ancestor collapsed on the point of death. A band of Yanktonais Sioux discovered him and nursed him back to health. François stayed with the band for the rest of his life and became a valued member of the tribe because he could speak French, a commonly used trade language on the river.

An old winter count of the Lower Yanktonais Dakota known as the John K. Bear count includes this fact for the year 1785: "Dakota *winyan wan wasicun hiknayan*," or

"Dakota woman married a white man." In James Howard's commentary on this winter count, he suggests that the man was a French Canadian *coureur du bois*, or fur trader. I have always liked to believe that this man was my ancestor and that this notation marked his entrance into the Sioux Nation. Of course, there is no way of verifying this match. But my ancestor did stay among the Lower Yanktonais, did marry into the tribe, and had a son, François Xavier, who was born around the same date.

The Yanktonais bands roamed up and down the river from around present-day Yankton, South Dakota, to near Devil's Lake in North Dakota. The westernmost bands often crossed the river and aligned themselves with the Hunkpapa, Two Kettles, and Blackfeet bands of Teton Sioux for hunting, horse stealing, and trading. What is certain is that François Xavier, when he was of age, did court and marry during a year when the Yanktonais were living with these other bands. He married Mazaicunwin, a prominent woman from a good family from the Blackfeet band of Tetons. They had at least three children. Mary was born in 1802, Julia in 1804. A son, François, who was my great-grandfather, was born in 1816. The children were three-quarters Sioux and were raised in the traditional Sioux ways. Julia, who lived until the age of ninety-three, became an important part of my grandfather's life since she could tell him what had happened long before his father was born. She died in 1897.

In 1819 there was apparently a des Lauriers Island just below the Big Bend; François Xavier might have established a trading post there at an early date. No records indicate how the island got its name, but a French settlement did exist there long before Fort Tecumseh (later Fort Pierre) was established further north on the river. Perhaps another child of François Xavier returned to his French heritage and became a trader. There were a few people of that name in St. Louis. Francis Parkman describes a rather surly individual named Deloriers who took care of Parkman's pack animals on his journey west. A Deslauriers is briefly listed as a partner in one of Pierre Choteau's companies on the Missouri, but he is hardly significant as a historical figure. It appears that there were many members of this family active in all kinds of occupations during the first several decades of the nineteenth century.

*   *   *   *

The Yanktonais could not pronounce "François," and so they reversed the sounds and called him "Saswe." Hereafter I will use this name for my great-grandfather, to keep the identification of family members clear. His name appears on the treaty monument at Greenwood, South Dakota, as Frank Deloria, and in Washington, D.C., he signed the 1858 Yankton treaty as Cecahinna or "Hairy Legs"—his French blood seems to have asserted itself in that manner.

He is the chief with the big warbonnet in the famous picture of the Indian delegations who went to the White House to see President Andrew Johnson in 1868 to renegotiate the treaty. The group is posed on the patio and second-story railing of the White House. Saswe is the only person wearing a warbonnet in the picture. Later he sat for a photograph at a studio in Washington.

In 1828, when Saswe was twelve, the family traveled to a big gathering of the Yanktonais bands at the Big Bend of the Missouri. The bands usually gathered in the spring to allocate hunting grounds for the season, and it was a time for courting, visiting, and celebration. Later some bands would go north and join Teton bands while others would go south

Sioux Indians on a visit to President Andrew Johnson at the White House, 1868. Saswe is shown wearing a warbonnet. Author's collection.

to the Platte to hunt buffalo, steal horses from the Pawnees and Poncas, and trade with the whites.

A group of boys of Saswe's band challenged the boys of another band to a game of shinny, a kind of field hockey played by the Sioux in those days. His team lost and so they treated the winners to a feast and it lasted until quite late. Saswe came home very late from these activities. With little more than a new moon, it was very difficult to see. As he lifted the flap of the tipi to enter, a voice called his name clearly three times. He paused in the entrance, undecided whether or not to go back to where the people were feasting. But as he looked around to see who had called him, he found that the crowd had dwindled away. Most people had disappeared into their tipis to sleep and no one was to be found. He thought someone was playing a joke on him so he went into the tipi and went to sleep.

The following year found the Yanktonais bands again gathered together at approximately the same locale. Saswe, now thirteen years old, had started to assume the role and duties of an adult. He had hunted buffalo with the grown men and had gone on several horse-stealing raids against the Pawnees in the Nebraska area. He had not accomplished anything of note but was included in the campfires where the old men told stories and encouraged the boys to aspire to be warriors and good hunters. This year he stayed at a campfire, listening to the elders and talking with other boys the same age.

Again he returned late to his parents' tipi. Just before he ducked his head under the tipi flap, he again heard his name called clearly three times. The voice sounded the same as the voice he had heard the previous year. So the next day he sought out the older medicine men and told them of his experiences. After listening patiently, they told him to reflect on these experiences, and if he had the same experience the next year, he should plan to do a vision quest. For a year he reflected in odd moments on this voice that had called him. Try as he might, he could not invoke any voices or messages. His life was otherwise devoid of any supernatural experiences and so he finally gave up thinking about the two times he had been called. The third year there was no gathering of Yanktonais and his band was camped near Choteau Creek, an area later included within the Yankton Reservation. At about the same time of year, which I estimate as mid-May, a day or so after the new moon, he again heard the voice calling him. It was strong and commanding, and he walked around the camp circle trying to discover whether he was being tricked by his friends. But he found no one awake. He spent the remainder of the night thinking about what had happened. When this experience was repeated the following year, Saswe determined to go on a vision quest at his first opportunity.

Shortly after the fourth experience, the Yanktonais band decided to go north to hunt with the Blackfeet, Hunkpapas, and other Yanktonais in the area now occupied by the Standing Rock Reservation. When the band was a few miles north of Pierre, the family decided to break away from the band and go to a high butte near present-day Blunt, South Dakota, where Saswe could do his vision quest. Since François Xavier often allowed his wife to visit her people in the summertime, it happened that no adult men were in the party. Saswe's mother, sisters, aunts, and cousins were the only adults in the group. The family planned to ride hard after Saswe had done his vision quest to catch the rest of the band when they crossed the Missouri.

They made camp in a draw northeast of the butte. The next day Saswe took his pipe and went up to the top of the hill to pray. He stood up on the butte praying, occasionally lighting and offering a pipe to the spirits in a location where he would be visible to the people in the camp. When my father and I walked that butte in 1986, we found a prayer pit where these rituals were performed and it was within sight of where the people must have camped.

Saswe stood there praying and lamenting, night and day, for two days without food or water. But sometime in the mid-afternoon of the third day when the people in camp looked up at the hill, he was no longer visible. His mother became frightened. Since physical collapse was not uncommon during this kind of ritual, she asked his cousin Brown Bear to get his horse and go see if Saswe had fainted. Brown Bear mounted his horse and went around to the northwest side of the butte where the ground has a gradually sloping incline and is relatively easy to ascend.

As Brown Bear rode his horse forward it became very skittish, reared up, and tried to turn back. Brown Bear urged the horse forward but it simply circled in one place, stepping very gingerly, and trying to go back down the hill. Brown Bear looked down and there at the horse's feet, close enough to strike, was a large rattlesnake. He looked around for a path away from the snake and saw dozens of rattlesnakes moving across the grass in front of him. Brown Bear realized that he was completely surrounded by hundreds of the snakes. He began to lose nerve as he realized that the butte was probably the location of a large den of rattlers and that Saswe had made a very bad choice of places to do his quest.

However, Brown Bear was determined to see what had happened to his cousin. Using his rope, he lashed at the snakes and opened a path and rode several hundred feet forward to see if he could locate Saswe. There in the distance he saw a large bundle of snakes furiously writhing back and forth over Saswe's prostrate body. He figured that Saswe had fainted earlier and the snakes, finding his warm body, had swarmed over him, biting him so many times that they had killed him. He watched the body for a while and there was no sign of life.

Brown Bear then began singing a wailing lament and turned his horse, making his way back down the butte and returning to the camp. After telling his aunt, Saswe's mother, what he had seen, Brown Bear dismounted and sat exhausted and shaking, relieved that he had come down from the butte without suffering a similar fate from snake bites. The women immediately began wailing and cutting their hair and gashing their arms with knives, as was the custom when someone died. Since Saswe was the only boy in the family, his loss was taken very hard and the little party was inconsolable.

In the midst of this lamenting, Saswe walked into the camp, frightening everyone, since people had believed him to be dead. At first they thought that his ghost had come to say goodbye, and this belief only caused them more grief and fright. But Saswe called to them, said that he wasn't a ghost, and asked them to stop mourning. Brown Bear quickly asked how he had come through the swarm of rattlesnakes that were on the butte, and Saswe expressed great surprise at the question. He replied that he had seen no snakes or animals and that he was a little surprised that no birds, snakes, or other animals had come to visit him when he began his vision quest, as was to be expected in this ritual.

The women became terribly angry with Brown Bear, accusing him of failing to go up the hill to check on Saswe and making up the story of the snakes as an excuse for his cowardice. Brown Bear refused to admit that he had misrepresented the situation. Until the end of his life he insisted that he had been blocked by hundreds of rattlesnakes. When they later checked the north part of the hill for hoof prints, they did discover the area where Brown Bear had to use his whip on his horse.

On the southern part of that butte, in the old days, there was a long twisting trail of rocks arranged to resemble a rattlesnake. Some of the rocks can be seen today, although people have vandalized the spot, making the snake effigy difficult to discern. Later in his life, Saswe confirmed Brown Bear's story, although some female family members always felt that the snakes were just an excuse. When my father and I walked the butte in 1986, he remarked that he was happy it was a cold October day and we would not meet any snakes. I was standing behind him looking at several garter snakes and praying that we wouldn't encounter a rattler.

Saswe later related some of his vision experience to tribe and family members. He told almost no one about the middle part of his experience, as it pertained to specific information about the future of the Yanktonais. Apparently he was told not to reveal this information. His later actions would suggest that he acted on the information given him in the vision at critical periods of his life. He later had other visions as part of his career as a holy man, and these additional visions enabled him to become a competent healer and someone who could predict future events. But the first vision defined much of what subsequently happened to our family.

As Saswe would recall his experience for my grandfather and the other medicine men, he did not remember fainting but suddenly found himself in a country that he did not recognize. He was in a beautiful valley in the middle of which was a bare road, made apparently by a party of Indians whose travois had scraped away the grass, leaving a dirt track. As he was walking along he came to a large black tipi sitting in the middle of the road and so situated that he could not go around it. Recognizing that this encounter was something holy, he went into the tipi. Inside, the road continued for a short distance and forked, one branch going to the left and the other to the right. The two tracks continued. Saswe saw that there was no back to the tipi and the landscape seemed to stretch out forever. But at the same time there really *was* a back to the tipi—this made the tipi impossibly large and indicated to him that, having once entered, he could not go back.

On the left-hand road facing him were four human skeletons lined up in a row, extending a good distance down the track. These skeletons were seated with their legs bent, their upper torsos leaning forward, and their forearms resting on their knees. They were looking down at the road. On their arm and leg bones were tied large bundles of grass. As he looked from the skeletons to the road ahead, he saw that the road appeared chalky white. Taken together with the skeletons, it looked rather ordinary and unexciting. The road on the right was blood red. Looking down this road, Saswe saw four purification tents, small, black, and somber.

At the end of the white, left-hand road sat a large black hawk who moved his head almost continually side to side and looked intently at Saswe. On the right-hand fork at the end of the road and opposite the black hawk was a white owl. He stared straight ahead, also looking intently at Saswe.

After some time the hawk spoke to him, saying that he had to make a decision about the course of his life, that he must look carefully at the two roads. When he had made his choice, the meanings would be made clear to him. (In Plains Indian visions, the four skeletons and four tents would be understood to represent four generations of descendants who would be bound by this choice.)

Saswe stood for a long time trying to see what the respective roads, with the skeletons and tents, would tell him. Finally he motioned to the right, then took several steps on the red road. At that point the owl turned and said to the Hawk: "I knew he would take that road. You'd better come over here as he will need all the help he can get." The hawk walked over to where the owl was sitting. They told Saswe they would now explain what kind of life he had chosen.

Had he chosen it, the left-hand road with the four skeletons would have meant that Saswe would have four generations of prosperous descendants, but the people following him would be no more than skeletons with flesh who would contribute virtually nothing to the world. It would have been a safe but completely nondescript family that nonetheless would have luck and would prosper.

The red road, on the other hand, was fraught with danger but filled with life. The four purification tents meant that Saswe would kill four men of his own tribe and have to undergo four purification rituals. He would have great powers as a medicine man, the Thunders would be his close friends, and many birds and animals would help him. He was given a special stone to make it rain.

The owl then instructed Saswe to have moccasins made with a black hawk on the right foot and a white owl on the left foot. This order is, of course, the reverse of the position of the birds within the tipi, but it is the correct position when viewed from the spiritual world. Saswe wore these moccasins when he was going to use his spiritual powers. He would sit absolutely still and have people put a bundle of sticks in his mouth so that it would be impossible for him to talk or make any noise except a gurgling sound. Then he would flex his right foot and the loud screeching of a hawk would ring out but no hawk would be visible. When he flexed his left foot, an owl would hoot loudly. When he flexed both moccasins at the same time, the birds would cry out loudly and continually, causing his audience to take him seriously if only to avoid the noise. These birds, the owl said, would always be protective of Saswe and his descendants, and in times of crisis they would appear as a sign that the spirits were assisting them.

As previously mentioned, the middle part of Saswe's vision was only revealed to a few people, and none of the narrative or substance of it has come down through the family. My aunt Ella Deloria knew part of it but refused to tell anyone else in the family. The end of the vision found Saswe lifted off the butte and taken to the clouds. There he met a long line of Sioux warriors who identified themselves as the "Thunders." They were all mounted on black horses that were prancing around, ready to run. Saswe mounted a horse and asked the riders what was going to happen. They said they were waiting for the signal to ride and they were going to the "Big Water," which was the name of the Atlantic Ocean.

Suddenly there was a tremendous crack of thunder, and the line of riders spurred their horses and began charging forward as fast as the horses could run. They rode toward the eastern edge of the cloud but Saswe said that the cloud was always ahead of them—no matter how fast they rode, they could not leave the cloud. This experience is hauntingly like the ride of Black Elk at the end of his vision, and I suspect that many Sioux who became friends of the Thunders had the same experience. As the riders rode furiously toward the east, thunder and lightning would sporadically issue from the cloud, hitting the ground with a great roar. Finally they could see the Atlantic Ocean. Just as they reached the shoreline, the warriors reined in their horses and their journey ended.

As the horses milled around at the end of the trip, Saswe suddenly found himself in the shape of a yellow canary. When he looked around, he discovered that all the warriors had become different kinds of birds. For a while the birds enjoyed themselves, flying around and swooping, gliding, and diving in the air in a carefree manner. But soon they formed into flocks of each kind of bird and began their return trip to the west.

As they flew along, Saswe noticed that the different flocks would break away and return to earth. He said that when they reached the Mississippi, he noticed he could no longer see the other flights of birds, only the few canaries around him. Finally he was alone, heading for a butte, where he saw a prostrate figure on the ground. In his final moment as a bird, he found himself diving straight into the back of the person on the ground and felt a tremendous "thud" as he hit right between the shoulders. He came to consciousness again and lay on the ground for a long time catching his breath. At last he got up. Seeing that it was twilight, he hurried back down the hill to the camp.

*   *   *   *

If the story ended there, it would be a good narrative of a profound spiritual experience. But while Saswe was doing his vision quest something happened about sixty miles southwest of the butte that puzzled everyone who heard about it. In another camp of Yanktonais, a young woman had a dream in which she was standing near their camp on a butte located just north of present-day Reliance, South Dakota. She was looking north and saw three crows fly by. Their presence filled her with a feeling of danger.

Looking beyond the crows on the far horizon, she saw a middle-aged man standing on the medicine butte near what is now Blunt, South Dakota, looking toward her. He stared at her, then looked at the birds and shook his head sorrowfully. She asked if the birds signified that she would be in danger soon. He indicated that within three days she would be exposed to a great danger. Then she awoke.

The Yanktonais were camped a short distance from the Missouri River on high ground where they would be able to spot an enemy war party approaching them. On the third day after the dream an old woman approached the dreamer and asked her to go down to the Missouri shore and pick chokecherries with her. The young woman tried her best to beg off, but the old woman was insistent. After telling their relatives what they were going to do, they left the camp and headed for the Missouri. The river was a short distance away but out of sight and hearing of the people in the camp.

They had been picking the fruit for a short time when three Arickaras sprang from the bushes and grabbed the women. They had come south along the river on a horse-stealing expedition and believed that the women had seen them and might alert the Yanktonais. The young woman dropped her bag of chokecherries, broke loose from the Arickara holding her, and began swiftly running down the sandy shoreline.

Catching the men by surprise, she was able to put a little distance between herself and them, but she could hear their hard breathing and felt them rapidly gaining on her. Stooping as she ran, she grabbed a handful of sand and hastily threw it over her shoulder hoping to blind the nearest one and cause him to falter. Suddenly she could hear the men stop, as if they were breaking off the chase. Looking back, she could not see anyone on the shoreline. She ran even faster, thinking they had taken to the hillside to cut her off before she could reach the camp. She made it back to the Yanktonais camp and warned the men, who promptly grabbed their weapons and went to find the Arickaras. But they had disappeared, leaving the old woman dead.

Almost a year later the Arickaras visited the Yanktonais camp during a period of peace between the two groups. One of the men who had been on the horse-stealing expedition happened to glance up at the Sioux woman who was bringing his food and saw that it was the young woman they had chased. Since the tribes were at peace, he told the story from their point of view. He was within a few steps of grabbing the young woman, he said, when she threw sand in his face and vanished—not a trance of her was to be found. He wanted to know how she had disappeared right in front of their eyes. The story of this mysterious occurrence was told and retold for years by the two tribes. Some years later the young woman met Saswe—now much older—and identified him as the man she had seen in her dream.

Saswe became a very powerful medicine man as he grew older. The spirits gave him a special stone, a piece of granite that was circular and resembled a core from an oil drill except that it was very thin. It seemed so ordinary that one would overlook it if searching for a stone that could be a religious object. With this stone he could bring rain because of his relationship with the Thunders. He only had to get the stone wet to bring on the clouds and thunder.

My grandfather inherited the stone and always kept it with him to help ward off bad weather. One time when he was leading a group of his parishioners in a wagon train to attend the Niobrara Convocation, things got out of hand. The Niobrara Convocation, begun in 1872 at Santee, was the annual gathering of the Episcopalian Sioux during which the people reported on their church activities. It was modeled after the old gathering of the people at Bear Butte and was one of the few times that the Sioux could leave their reservations and visit other Sioux. Caravans of churchgoers in wagons, accompanied by an Indian policeman with a signed pass for the party, journeyed to a different reservation each year for this meeting. My grandfather looked forward to taking his people to the convocation since he had relatives on many of the reservations and he could visit them.

My grandfather's party had crossed the Cheyenne River on their way south to the Yankton Reservation when he accidentally got the stone wet. He hastily gathered the people together and told them that within a short time they would be subjected to an intense thunderstorm because of the accident with the stone. The people moved their wagons into a draw, drove stakes in the ground to tie them down, and moved their horses on down the draw where they could get maximum shelter from the storm. A massive tornado accompanied by a severe thunderstorm swept through the area shortly thereafter and nearly destroyed the group. Had they not been prepared for it, they would all have been killed.

Medicine men in those days had a set of superficial tricks that they did in public exhibitions of their powers. In his books on the Sioux, Standing Bear described some of the things they did to demonstrate their particular talents, such as allowing people to shoot at them without causing any apparent harm. Saswe would put a red-hot poker into his mouth, close his mouth tightly, and gradually pull out the poker. He would then tell the people to feel it. It was always cold after having been untouchably hot only moments before.

Miss Olden quoted my grandfather at length about Saswe's healing powers:

Saswe possessed an extraordinary gift of healing. In those days there was a man in camp who had a deep-seated rheumatic affliction. His joints were swollen, and he was constantly in pain and doubled up with the disease. The medicine man (Saswe) told him that he should never again eat the entrails of an animal or the gizzard of a bird; if he did he would surely die. The man obeyed and was completely cured.

A long while afterward, when the insides of an animal and of a bird were being prepared, this man thought he would like some to eat. His wife said to him: "Did not the medicine man tell you that if you ever again ate any of this you would die?" "Oh," replied her husband, "that was many years ago." Then he himself roasted a part of the entrails and the gizzard; shortly after eating them he died in great agony.

One day, while he was meditating in the fields, [Saswe] saw a vision. Some figures appeared and motioned to him to go with them; but he could not move, as he had become quite helpless in body. His spirit accompanied them to a *black house*, a dreary place, in which was "all manner of sickness and all manner of disease." Of the many people lying about in such distress, some were dying; but when Saswe touched them they sat up, quite reanimated and revivified, and many of them were permanently recovered. This black house or lodge appeared, afterward, to be a dark cloud filled with strange figures. (*The People of Tipi Sapa*, pp. 7–8)

Ella Deloria said that the place Saswe went to in the vision was the House of the Dead and that he was made to walk up and down a long enclosure and observe the various kinds of sicknesses that would kill people. After he had walked along observing the illnesses, he was told to pick several and he would be given the power to heal people who suffered from them. But he could only use these healing powers for the specific diseases he had chosen. He was told that he would lose his powers if he tried to heal someone with a disease he was not empowered to cure.

When he was small, my grandfather Tipi Sapa went with Saswe to assist in his healings. My grandfather told the family of several occasions when Saswe spent a short time with a sick person and then abruptly took his medicine bag and left, telling the grieving relatives that he could not heal the person and that they should get someone who could heal that sickness. Or he would simply state that the person was going to die regardless of any attempted cure.

Another of his healing accomplishments was recorded in St. Elizabeth's School's promotional material, indicating that Saswe's healings were still well known in 1917:

> Once he was called to help a woman with a wandering mind. He had her placed alone in a tipi, while her relatives insured perfect silence by keeping the dogs still. All night long he sang to the spirits, praying for their help. The evil spirit fluttered about the tent poles all night. In the morning he sent a spirit of thunder and lightning around the inside of her tent and her mind was restored.

Through spending a lot of time in isolation praying and speaking with the spirits, Saswe developed an intimate relationship with the Thunder spirits. One time, a white man, one of the first to live in the Yankton area, taunted Saswe about his powers, saying that he was just a fake. He said that Saswe should stand in a metal wash tub and hold an iron crowbar toward the sky during the next thunderstorm to demonstrate that he really had influence with the Thunders. The white man proposed that if Saswe was killed, he would inherit Saswe's favorite gray horse. Saswe made him a counter offer. He said that the white man didn't have to do anything. He could be wherever he liked during the next thunderstorm. Saswe would just tell the Thunders to search him out and kill him. The bet was quickly cancelled.

My cousin Phil Lane preserved a story about the killing of a white buffalo by a Yankton Sioux riding Saswe's horse. To my knowledge, it is the only story preserved about such an event. The man was much younger and more agile than Saswe but knew that the horse was well trained for hunting. When the white buffalo was discovered everyone rode after him, but only Saswe's horse could stand the pace of the chase. He outran all the other hunters and enabled the man to kill the white buffalo. When the white buffalo was brought back to the Yankton camp, Saswe gave a great feast. He brought out a necklace made of large bear claws, a very valuable thing. The people led the horse around the camp, singing songs extolling his stamina. Then Saswe put the necklace around the horse's neck and announced that the horse would never be ridden again in honor of the buffalo. He renamed the horse "Eagle Claws."

Although most of these stories are known primarily among family members, it is startling to find them verified in written sources as well. In volume XIV of the South Dakota Historical Collections, in an article entitled "Tales of the Dakota," is found a description of an incident illustrative of Saswe's powers:

Saswe, 1868. A portrait taken in Washington, D.C., during the renegotiation of the 1858 treaty. Author's collection.

Saswe was with a large number of Sioux camped on the east shore of the Missouri when their provisions utterly failed and they appealed to the medicine man for help. He then called the hunters and told them, "There are two hills near the present town of Eureka, with a lake lying south of them. Go at once, for two herds of buffalo will be coming between the hills. Do not delay, for this afternoon there will be a great blizzard and seven men of another party will be frozen to death." The hunters found the two herds as directed and secured an abundance of meat. The blizzard came promptly and seven men hunting these herds perished. (p. 494)

Saswe could perform the *yuwipi* ceremony, which is often used to find things. I suspect that the performance of this ceremony was omitted in this account of the incident. *Yuwipi* generally required that the medicine man be wrapped tightly in skins (later in blankets) and bound with strong ropes. He would then be left alone to consult with the spirits. In a very short time he would call to the people to come hear what the spirits had told him. They would find him sitting quietly, the skins and ropes all nicely folded and ready to use again.

Miss Olden included this incident in the original book, with this song, which Saswe sang to locate the buffalo:

SONG OF SASWE
I send my voice upward,
Telling the Good Spirit to come down;
So he comes down and tells me
What I want (him to tell me)

SASWE, ODOWAN KIN

Tchand pteatan wait cau-han aliyeya ecee kin dee,
Waukankiya hoye wayacan,
Nari ksapa e wakidowan ye,
Wakidowan cauhan tiyata hiye,
Na taku wan waein kin he hosi hi ecer

*   *   *   *

Saswe married a prominent woman of the Blackfeet
Sioux band, Sihasapawin—or Blackfeet Woman. She was the
daughter of Bear Foot, a famous chief, and sister of the famous
chief Mad Bear and his brothers, Walks in the Wind and
Tiger. Marrying into a band so far away guaranteed that no
close blood relationship existed between the couple. It also
meant that Saswe and his family would often travel up and
down the Missouri so that his wife could spend time with her
family. They had six children: Tasunkeoyedutawin (Alice),
Tunkanicagewin (Anna), Wakancekiyewin (Sarah), Tipi
Sapa (Philip, my grandfather), Ziwina (Carrie), and
Tasunkawakanwin (Euphrasia). Three of the children, Alice,
Sarah, and Philip, were born on the Grand River in northern
South Dakota, suggesting that Saswe's band quite frequently
visited the Hunkpapas and Blackfeet Sioux.

Since Saswe was a prosperous medicine man, he had
two other wives, Tatedutawin and Anpetuicagapinwin, by
whom he had seven other children who were listed in the
Yankton Mission register. Inquiring among the many people
descended from Saswe, I was told that he had twenty-two
children, eighteen girls and four boys. Perhaps only those
children who lived near him on the Yankton Reservation
and were baptized by the Episcopal missionary had their
names and birth places recorded.

Continued contact with an increasing number of fur traders convinced Saswe that the times were changing and that the white man's invasion was not a passing phenomenon. Sometime after the birth of my grandfather in 1853, Saswe moved his families down to the Missouri near present-day Lake Andes, South Dakota, and began to cut and sell wood to steamboats traveling up river. His camp was located directly across the river from Fort Randall at what became known as White Swan Landing. Eventually Saswe became the recognized leader of one of the smaller Yankton bands that was related to Chief White Swan, who headed the western division of the tribe.

In this capacity Saswe was chosen as one of the seven Yankton chiefs to go to Washington to negotiate the 1858 treaty. This treaty ceded large portions of southeastern South Dakota and set aside a comfortable reservation along the Missouri for the Yanktons. This responsibility was given him in spite of the fact that he was a Yanktonais, a group of bands once closely related to the Yanktons but now separate from them. Compared with the Yanktons, he was really just a visitor. Normally he would have lived far to the north with the Yanktonais, who were allied with the Hunkpapas and Blackfeet Sioux.

During his visit to Washington, Saswe was interviewed by people at the Bureau of Indian Affairs. He gave them a small leather packet that he wore around his neck as a good luck charm. It had been passed down in the family for at least three generations. When the packet was opened it was discovered that it contained a set of personal papers identifying the young French boy who had been on the fur-trading expedition to Lake Winnipeg. After the papers were translated, the band Saswe headed was called the "Half-Breed Band"— and recorded as such in many government papers—because of Saswe's French blood, although most of the band were full-bloods and Saswe himself was three-quarters Sioux.

*   *   *   *

Saswe did commit the four murders that were predicted in his vision. In the early 1850s his sister came to him one day terribly beaten and bleeding and complained that her husband had been very abusive to her. My father always said that her husband made her walk on thistles and hot coals to punish her. When he saw the physical condition of his sister, Saswe loaded his shotgun, walked over to their tipi, and promptly dispatched his brother-in-law with a shot to the body. If there had been any public abuse of his sister similar to what my father described, Saswe would have acted immediately without any complaint from his sister.

The next two murders occurred in a unique set of circumstances. After the Sioux had been dispersed from Minnesota in the 1862 war, General Alfred Sully came to the Yanktons and demanded that they surrender any Santee Sioux who might be hiding in their camps and that the Yanktons guarantee they would remain peaceful and not join in the combat. At that time there was a terrible scare among the whites near Yankton, South Dakota, and it took some very fast talking by the Army officers at Fort Randall to keep the Yanktons from joining the Minnesota Sioux bands' struggle.

The Yankton chiefs discovered that four Santees were hiding in their camps. They didn't know what to do with them. Sully had hired about sixty Yanktons as scouts against the Santees, and it would not be long before the Santees' presence would be known. With so many Yanktons working for the U.S. Army while others were sympathetic to the Santees, it appeared that the tribe might split into warring factions unless some decision was made quickly about these men. After a prolonged council, the chiefs decided that if they killed two of the four men and reported it to Sully, they would have shown their loyalty to the United States. That they had not surrendered all four might mitigate some of the tension that would arise with their Santee cousins.

No one would volunteer to kill the two men, however, and the debate went on for hours. Finally, Saswe got up and told of his vision and the fact that he was told that he would murder four Sioux during his life. Saswe felt that the situation, although painful, had been predicted in his vision. He said he would do it since he was a Yanktonais and did not have close relatives among the Yankton bands who might take offense at the killings.

Saswe got his gun and rode out to where the Santees were being kept. He walked into the enclosure, pulled out his pistol, and shot two of the men. He turned his pistol over to one of the other chiefs and walked out the entrance. He paid a crier, a person who announced the public notices of the tribe, to ride around the camp and tell of the killings. He then said that he would go to the top of a nearby hill, without weapons, and sit for a day and a night. The crier announced that Saswe wanted any relatives or friends of the two murdered men who wanted to take his life to ride up the hill and kill him any time during this period. He would not try to defend himself.

Fearful for his son Philip's life, Saswe had friends and cousins spirit Philip and two cousins away to the woods and hide them until the time had expired. My grandfather was ten years old at the time and remembered the tensions in the camp all his life.

It seemed unlikely to me, when I was a boy, that the saintly old man in the warbonnet could have done such a thing. I had always thought the story was fictional. Many years later as I was reading the memoirs of an old pioneer woman published in 1892, I was surprised to discover the following:

About this same time [during the Minnesota war] some of the scouts captured another rover; and on that occasion they held a council to see what they better do with him. They thought they were in power to shoot him. One of them said: "We were ordered to take these men and make prisoners of them, but the commander refuses to take them after we catch them." Just then an old Indian, DeLurio, called 'Chief-of-the-half-breeds,' rode up and said: "If you don't know what to do with that Indian, I do!" and instantly drew up and shot him dead in his seat. (Frances Chamberlain Holley, *Once Their Home*, p. 77)

These killings occurred thirty years before the book was written, indicating that Saswe's activities had been common knowledge among both Indians and whites for more than a generation and that, although Mrs. Holley had misunderstood the circumstances of the killings, the story had been a familiar one on the Dakota frontier.

The fourth killing occurred when Saswe was getting on in years. Again it was a case of wife abuse, this time when a man beat one of Saswe's daughters and sent her home crying. With considerably more daughters than sons, Saswe was determined to hold his extended family together, and this killing was explained in the family as a case of protecting his grandchildren as much as protecting his daughter. This story was also known far and wide and was recorded by Mrs. Holley:

To show what a man this DeLuris was for dispatch, an incident is related of a little family affair of his which took place just prior to the above deed. It seems that his daughter had married a man who inflicted great abuse upon her. DeLuris had

warned him several times that he must be careful
how he conducted himself, and one day it was
reported to him that his son-in-law had been whip-
ping his wife. The indignant father made no reply,
but mounted his pony and rode directly to the
lodge of his child. He hastily dismounted and
walked inside, saying: "My son-in-law, I have come
to kill you!" and without further comment or
explanation shot him. (p. 77)

The older members of our family believed that this incident occurred after Saswe killed the Santees and was the
final killing. The daughters of Sihasapawin would have been
very young in 1863 and probably not married until the
1870s. Saswe could well have killed his son-in-law while he
was settled on the reservation without encountering any real
trouble from the government.

*   *   *   *

At about age fifty-five, Saswe began to be bothered by
the ghosts of the men he had killed. During that period, he
had a little settlement on the banks of the Missouri with
three houses rather evenly spaced along the bank, one for
each wife. His cabin was in the center of the clearing,
about fifty feet in front of the women's cabins. The wives
would take turns coming to his cabin and taking care of
him for one month at a time. Generally he lived alone and
the women simply fed him and made certain that his cabin
was clean and warm.

Since he was becoming physically impaired and could no
longer go out on long vision quests, Saswe began to do more
yuwipi ceremonies. He would have people wrap him tightly in

buffalo robes inside his cabin and bind him with rawhide ropes. They would leave him alone and the spirits would come and consult with him. Within a short time he would come out to talk with people who were attending the ceremony. When they looked inside, they found the robes folded and stacked and the ropes tightly coiled. Through these ceremonies, Saswe would locate lost things and give prophecies of the future. He had both Indian and whites as clients.

Despite his contact with the spirits, the hauntings grew worse. Saswe had ridden a cherished gray horse when he killed the two Santees. Every evening the horse would come down from the pasture on the hill and stand next to Saswe's cabin all night. Saswe said that the ghosts of the men were bothering the horse and the animal needed to feel he was within the circle of Saswe's protection. Then Saswe began to see the faces of the men he had killed whenever he would try to drink any liquids. They would appear as reflections, taunting him and uttering threats only he could hear. Saswe consulted the other Yankton medicine men about a cure for this condition, but no one was able to help him.

He began to search out the missionaries to discuss with them how he could rid himself of this curse. While the missionaries did not have an answer, he saw that they represented the kind of life that the Yanktons would have to live in the future. It was becoming increasingly clear to Saswe that the old ways were gone, and now that the Yanktons were now restricted to a small tract of land, they would have to support themselves in the white man's way. So Saswe and three other Yankton chiefs asked the Episcopal missionary at the Santee Reservation across the river to begin church work on the Yankton Reservation. After much debate, the Episcopalians sent Dr. Joseph Cook to minister to them.

When a church was set up, Saswe became a regular churchgoer. He began advising his son to consider the white man's religion. We have often wondered if Saswe saw this change as a partial fulfillment of his vision, since there was no doubt that he wanted Philip to follow a religious life but not necessarily the traditional Sioux religion.

Finally Saswe himself agreed to be baptized, and in 1873 he not only became a Christian but also formally married Sihasapawin, the Blackfeet Sioux woman, according to the white man's way. He stopping living with the other two wives, one of whom went back to her people at Crow Creek, where most of the Yanktonais were now settled.

He said that after his baptism when the people were having a feast to celebrate his conversion, he looked in his coffee cup and for the first time in years did not see any of the dead men's faces. When Saswe died in October 1876, he received prominent notice in one of the Episcopal Church newsletters as a faithful member of the new mission church and a help to the missionaries. For better or for worse, he had followed the path seen in his youthful vision forty-five years before. Some family members have speculated that the middle part of his vision forecast his eventual embrace of a new religion and that this was so distasteful to Saswe that he kept it a secret and simply let events unfold.

*   *   *   *

I have saved one example of his spiritual powers until last because it had a direct bearing on my grandfather and was not known outside the family for a long time. In 1856, when Philip was about three years old, Saswe had to go on a long trip. When he returned, the women were all wailing and mutilating themselves and he knew that a relative had died. When he asked the women they cried harder and ran away from him. He entered his tipi and found my grandfather laid out on a buffalo robe. He had caught a fever and, in spite of the best the people could do, had passed away the day before Saswe returned.

Saswe stayed inside the cabin for a long time. People heard his terrible cries of grief but no one dared to go in and talk with him. He had named my grandfather Tipi Sapa— Black Lodge—as a dedication to his vision of the black tipi he had entered. Now, with the death of his little boy, his hopes seemed to be futile. Saswe finally emerged from the tipi, his arms and legs bloody with knife wounds of grief, carrying Philip's body in his arms. He mounted his horse and rode off to a high hill, where he dismounted and began to pray. All night and all the next day he sat there singing laments with the boy's body in his arms.

My father told me that Saswe spoke very gruffly with the Thunders. He boldly said that he had done everything they had asked and told them that they could take anything of his except that boy. He pleaded that they return him. Just about sundown the people looked anxiously toward the hill, wondering if Saswe was going to spend another night and day there, and also wondering how they would get Tipi Sapa's body away from him so they could proceed with the burial.

To their surprise they saw Saswe walking hand in hand with Tipi Sapa, the gray horse trailing behind them. No one spoke a word as the two walked into the tipi and sat down. Finally, one of the women prepared some food and broth for them and the spell was broken. My father said that after this demonstration of his powers, people in the band became very afraid of Saswe. Among his relatives there was a strong sense of alienation because it was obvious that Saswe greatly favored Tipi Sapa.

Reverend Philip Deloria at Niobrara Convocation, 1916. Author's collection.

Tipi Sapa

We come now to the life of my grandfather, Tipi Sapa, later Philip Joseph Deloria. He was born on the Grand River in northern South Dakota on Christmas Day in 1853. Saswe and Sihasapawin had remembered that he was born on a new moon. When he was baptized, the missionary traced the dates back to find out what day that would have been and was pleasantly surprised to discover it was Christmas. The Yanktonais band was visiting with the Blackfeet; since Sihasapawin was of that band, she had apparently come home to have her baby.

My grandfather related the circumstances of his birth, and Miss Olden included them in a short biography at the beginning of *The People of Tipi Sapa*, from which I quote below:

> Once upon a time, this woman made a prayer and vow to the Great Spirit. The result of this prayer was a baby boy to gladden the mother's heart and the happy woman fulfilled her vow by a performance of the "Thanksgiving Ceremony."
>
> The offering consisted of a buffalo robe richly worked with porcupine quills, a peacepipe, and a

small bag, also embroidered in porcupine quills, containing a lock of the mother's hair and a lock of the child's and carefully sealed. All these articles were tied into a small bundle and fastened to the tip of a pole which was erected within the tipi.

When all these preparations were accomplished, Blackfeet Woman called together the influential people of the tribe to her tipi and gave them a feast. At the conclusion of the feast, she lighted a pipe, presented it in turn to heaven, to the four winds, and to the earth and said:

"Great Spirit, I have asked you for a boy. You have given him to me. I am happy. I pray you accept my thanks and these gifts which I have prepared and am offering to you. May my son grow up. May he be useful. May he observe faithfully those laws and customs which we have observed, and our fathers before us."

When she had ended, her guests with one accord cried, "Ha ye" (So be it). Then the pole, with the offering still tied to it, was carried to a hill and planted there. People going by saw it, but did not touch it, for it was the Great Spirit's property. (*The People of Tipi Sapa*, pp. 2–4)

Philip went through all the traditional Sioux ceremonies for infants, including the piercing of his ears. In the short biography Miss Olden recorded Tipi Sapa's account of this ritual:

Saswe was the possessor of a famous and swift black horse, also a warbonnet and a handsome skin robe worked in beads and porcupine quills. He tied these articles in front of the horse, then sent for an old man to come and get them because the boy was born. When the old man arrived, Saswe said to him: "Take your knife and prick the child's ears on both sides, and [put] sharp lead against his ears every night until they are pierced through. That is the first thing done in honoring a son. He is to wear earrings. Tell the people this boy is to have the name of Tipi Sapa—Black Lodge."

The old man took the horse, with the war-bonnet and robe attached to him, and rode around in the circle, proclaiming the boy's name; then, every night for a time, he put sharp lead in the lobes of his ears. (*The People of Tipi Sapa*, pp. 8–9)

For some reason the cuts in the lobes were made very deep and wide, leaving rather ugly holes that healed badly. In later years people in church would sit and stare at his ears, and this embarrassed Philip immensely. But the novelty of the thing made him more popular with the white clergy and with eastern church congregations since it was living proof that the church had claimed a real prize.

When the Yankton Reservation was established in 1858 and the people settled down and began living in cabins, the tribe found itself at the center of many disputes. It took real statesmanship to remain neutral while their cousins to the east fought a hopeless war against the whites in 1862 and their kin to the west were closing the Bozeman Trail and fighting at various locations in Colorado, Wyoming, the Dakotas, and Montana. But the Yanktons were people with an elevated sense of honor, and they felt themselves obligated to remain at peace with the United States. Lewis and Clark had visited them in 1804 and wrapped the newborn

"Struck-by-the-Ree," a chief's son, in the American flag. Struck-by-the-Ree became the most influential chief of the Yanktons and always preferred to keep the peace because of this christening.

One of several boys amidst a bevy of sisters and half sisters, Philip was Saswe's favorite child and was always in tow when Saswe went to perform his religious and political duties. When Saswe began his healings, Philip accompanied him and later told my father and his sisters about the different ways that Saswe could heal people. Philip must have been horrified then when Saswe began to advise him to adopt the white man's way. Some fragments of family stories suggest that Philip reached his late teens wanting to be a warrior in the old way and went to great lengths to do the traditional things. He became attracted to Christianity in a strange way and eventually reversed his plans completely.

The story of my grandfather's conversion was a familiar one to several generations of Episcopalians, since it was publicized by missionary bishops and church headquarters in their campaigns to raise funds for the Indian missions. When he was about seventeen years old, Philip was riding to the agency and happened to go by the Episcopal Mission while they were singing a hymn: "Guide Me, O Thou Great Jehovah." The tune, as the Sioux sang it, was a dirge that could hardly have been comforting, but the song does remain with you after you hear it a couple of times.

According to Tipi Sapa's account:

> One day—it must have been Sunday—I was following a path which led by the little church. Out of the open window I heard the sound of voices. The tune they sang was pleasant to hear. I wanted to hear it again, to learn it if possible. So I

went up to the church on three successive Sundays but that tune was not sung. On the fourth Sunday, however, I was happy to hear the hymn I had longed for.

I stood next to a man who sang out of a book. From him I caught the words of the first verse and learned them by heart. When I left that church, able to carry the tune and sing the first verse of the Dakota translation of "Guide Me, O Thou Great Jehovah," I felt that I was the possessor of a great treasure. From that day on I attended the services with regularity, hoping to learn other things as beautiful as that hymn. (*The People of Tipi Sapa*, pp. 10–11)

His attendance brought him to the attention of Reverend Joseph Cook, who then worked hard to convert him:

One day after a service, Mr. Cook asked all the young men in the congregation to remain. After a few general remarks, he dismissed all of them but asked me to wait behind. You are to cut your hair short, dress like a white man and go to school. What is your feeling about it? I replied, very decidedly: "No!" Again and again he asked me, and as often I gave him the one answer.

In their teachings my father and mother had said so often: "A scalp lock of beautiful long hair is a most desirable thing for a warrior to possess. Take care of your hair. Be brave, and if an enemy gets your scalp lock, die like a man. He who dies uttering a cry is not a man, and is a disgrace to his people." I wanted to keep my hair long and beautiful as became a warrior.

Tipi Sapa (Philip Deloria) after his conversion to Christianity. He was made to cut his long hair and assume the dress of the white man. Author's collection.

Meantime Mr. Cook did not grow weary of talking to me, and finally I compared the two courses which lay ahead, the heathen life and the Christian life, and after much deliberation, I made my decision. Going to Mr. Cook I gave myself up, had my long hair cut off, and assumed the dress of the white man. It was far from easy to go back and face my people, many of whom were disappointed and jeered at me. "Coward! He fears warfare," "See, he chooses an easy life," and many similar taunts were thrown at me.

In the spring of 1871, Bishop Clarkson confirmed me. Afterward I went to Nebraska College for two years and the Shattuck School at Faribault, Minnesota, for one year. In spite of my ambition to get ahead, I was held back by pneumonia two successive years, so that I did not have three full years of school. In 1874 I returned to my people, equipped with the knowledge of reading, writing, and figuring, which I had been able to acquire. Almost immediately I became a lay reader in the Church, and at the same time assumed my duties as chief in the place of my father, having been given by the Indian Department a medal signifying my authority. (*The People of Tipi Sapa*, pp. 11–13)

That scenario has always been the official church interpretation of his conversion and was indeed the story that Philip himself told about his conversion. It seems more likely that Saswe, who had invited the Episcopalians to the reservation, had been talking with Tipi Sapa at home, urging him to adopt the new religion, since his vision had predicted that four generations of his family would assume religious

Standing Rock Reservation, South Dakota, 1890s. Author's collection.

responsibilities. Saswe's quick conversion when Tipi Sapa was baptized suggests that much theological discussion had gone on between father and son.

Philip was torn between serving his people as a chief and serving them as a priest. He admitted that he had a "great many temptations" to leave the religious life and devote himself to political leadership. But he finally resolved them:

> When I saw my way a littler clearer, I decided to lay aside my chieftainship and work for the spiritual uplift of my people. Accordingly, Bishop Hare admitted me to deacon on June 24, 1883.
>
> While I was in deacon's orders, Bishop Hare would say, "Pack up and go to such and such a place." I would go each time, and do the work I found there to be done. When in two or three years the work had progressed, quite unexpectedly he would ask me to go elsewhere. One day the Bishop said: "Pack up your things and go to Standing Rock." I came and I have been here ever since, through a period of twenty-six years. (*The People of Tipi Sapa*, pp. 13–14)

From the church records, which are scanty, it does appear that Philip was sent quite frequently to different reservations to do church work. We find him at Rosebud, Standing Rock, and Cheyenne River during the 1880s. Since Rosebud and Cheyenne River had Episcopal schools, he was probably filling in wherever the church needed teachers. But he was being overly modest in saying merely that the church work flourished. Years later the bishop would credit Tipi Sapa with being the major influence in building the Episcopal missions in South Dakota.

In 1875, Tipi Sapa had married Annie Brunot. He had every reason to believe that he was headed down a road of relative happiness. They had a boy, Francis Philip, in November 1876, a month after Saswe died, and in 1879 Annie gave birth to a little girl who lived about ten days. Tragically, Annie died about a month later from complications of childbirth. Shortly after Annie died, the Bishop sent Philip and his little boy to Rosebud, where Philip was to teach at St. Mary's School. Then the people of Band Eight re-elected him as chief because his knowledge of white society was needed by them in their dealings with the government.

Since he could not, on principle, turn down the position of chief of the band, Tipi Sapa took on a crushing burden of both church and tribal work. He had to teach school, take care of his small son, and make the long journey back to the Yankton Reservation to attend council meetings and listen to the people's complaints about the government. This trip would have been close to one hundred miles from Rosebud—much farther from other reservations—by horse and buggy. Bishop Hare expected Philip to devote all of his time and energies to church work and must not have been very happy when Philip agreed to become chief.

One of the things Philip accomplished during this time was the founding of the Planting Society. In those days prominent men would gather others together and form a society to perform charitable deeds on behalf of the poor and neglected members of the tribe or band. Sitting Bull in his prime started the Big Bellies, which was not a group of overweight people but rather a society composed of men pledged to take care of the poor. The bigness of belly represented the large concern they had for their people.

Philip, David Tatiyopa, and Baptiste Lambert were cofounders of the Planting Society, whose purpose was to encourage the people to settle down and begin to farm. In today's politically correct atmosphere such a goal would be considered a negative development since the contemporary style is to pretend that all our ancestors resisted the white man's culture and maintained their old traditions. That view is largely false.

With the destruction of the game by settlers, the government had to provide rations to feed the people under the provisions of several treaties. Rations were usually butchered beef, flour, bacon, and some kinds of canned goods. With massive theft of these goods by the agents, there was never enough food available to feed the people.

Realizing that annuities were insufficient and rarely paid on time and that hunting no longer provided a steady food supply, many Yankton families took up farming to feed themselves as best they could. Some of the more traditional people in the tribe refused to farm and often ran their horses over the gardens of those who were planting. So the society members placed themselves at considerable risk in this venture. But eventually most Yanktons became good farmers and horse breeders.

Planting was not the only concern of the society. Looking around at the various missionaries then seeking converts among the Sioux and seeing their intolerance of other denominations worried these men. Already the Catholics were fighting with the Protestants. Although the churches were all preaching peace and fellowship, the missionaries expected their converts to avoid the members of other churches.

Religious competition was splitting the Yanktons and Santees into religious cliques. Philip and his friends could see that the same process would happen wherever the missionaries made headway in converting the Sioux. So the

"Sioux Indians Getting Their Beef Rations," 1893. Nebraska State Historical Society, no. A597: 2-70. Photo by J. A. Anderson.

Niobrara Convocation. Episcopalian Sioux gathered in a camp circle near Holy Comforter Episcopal Church, Lower Brulé, July 26, 1895. Author's collection.

Planting Society began to evolve along religious lines. The members changed its name to the Brotherhood of Christian Unity (BCU) and recruited members from the Congregational, Presbyterian, and Episcopalian Sioux converts. The Catholics refused to allow their converts to join and continued to preach that the Protestants were going straight to hell.

The BCU gained a large membership in its first few decades because it was modeled after traditional ways of formalizing people's charitable instincts. It gradually became predominantly Episcopalian and Presbyterian since the Congregationalists made considerably fewer converts than the other churches. The BCU remained a viable group until the mid-1980s, when it was dissolved. It was in fact the only group that attempted to meet the special needs of people dealing with emergencies and family tragedies.

In 1880 Spotted Tail, the famous chief of the Brulé Sioux, gathered chiefs from the various agencies and led this delegation to Washington, D.C., and the Carlisle Indian School in Pennsylvania. Philip was one of the chiefs of the Yankton delegation headed by Struck-by-the-Ree to take this trip. The group toured the nation's capital, spent some time inspecting Carlisle, and returned home to report to the people how the government schools were educating the children. Spotted Tail, who abhorred physical discipline, saw the children harshly disciplined and demanded that his children be sent home. Struck-by-the-Ree did not see the incident or was not offended by it, and the Yanktons continued to send some of their children there.

In 1881 Philip married again to provide a home for his little boy. Jennie Lamont, a mixed-blood woman from the White Swan settlement at Yankton, became his second wife. Tragically, their happiness was disrupted in 1883 when Francis Philip died at the age of six, probably from tuberculosis. Jennie and Philip had two girls, Minerva, born in 1884, and Lyma, born in 1887. When Philip was transferred to Standing Rock, he acted first as a Helper, a layman's office created by Bishop Hare to give some status to influential men who helped with church work. Then he was ordained as a deacon, the first step toward becoming a priest and regular clergyman.

Again the same tragic pattern of death occurred. Jennie died shortly after giving birth to their second child. Philip was once again a widower with small children to support. Jennie's death must have created great doubts in Tipi Sapa about his conversion. It seemed reasonable to believe that the Christian god would bestow upon his followers some blessings. Saswe, after all, had been given healing and prophetic powers and protection. Yet Philip had lost two wives and two children and seemed to have a bleak future. It was difficult to extol the virtues of Christianity when it appeared that the converts suffered more than those who had rejected the new religion.

In 1888 Philip was placed in charge of the Episcopal missions on the South Dakota side of the Standing Rock Reservation, which straddled the border of what would a year later be two new states. He resided at St. Elizabeth's Church at Wakpala, which was the only Episcopal Church on the reservation. In 1892, a school named St. Elizabeth's was built three miles northeast of Wakpala. There is a bit of irony in Tipi Sapa's assignment that must be noted. When he was born, the Sioux were completely free and controlled the whole west river country of South Dakota. Philip was born about seven miles due south of St. Elizabeth's Mission on the Grand River. The bishop knew him only as a Yankton, since it was on that reservation that he first encountered our family. Since it was forbidden by church policy for a man to be assigned to minister to his own people, the Bishop assigned

St. Elizabeth's Mission, Standing Rock Reservation, Wakpala, South Dakota, in the 1890s. Author's collection.

Philip to Standing Rock, which was the farthest church mission from the Yankton Reservation—thus sending him home to his mother's people.

Some of Sitting Bull's people, after returning from Canada, had decided to camp near Wakpala. They were very friendly, attending the services and generally participating in the church activities of the little community. Many of them joined St. Elizabeth's. Philip's work was expanding quickly. As he developed congregations further west on the reservation, new little chapels were built. They became a regular part of his schedule of services. He sometimes would depart before dawn with his team of horses and wagon, go to a remote chapel to hold services, and hurry back to St. Elizabeth's at Wakpala for services there.

The people loved the opportunity to get together and visit. When the weather was good they would bring their teams and wagons and camp for three days near the church. The typical Sunday schedule at St. Elizabeth's began with Holy Communion in the late morning, then lunch, followed by a short break. In the mid-afternoon the people would have a business meeting of the men's and women's church societies, followed by a short break and evening prayer. The Sioux Christians were a good deal more serious about their religious commitments than were the whites.

As chapels continued to be established further west, Tipi Sapa would leave on a Saturday, hold the same exhausting schedule at one of the chapels, and return on Monday. About twenty-five miles north of Wakpala at Kenel were the camps of the Blackfeet Sioux and his uncles Mad Bear, Walks in the Wind, and Tiger. They were undergoing indoctrination as Roman Catholics, and the missionary refused to let them associate with Episcopalians. Bishop Hare was not too eager to have this fraternization either, so Philip could only see his relatives on secular public occasions such as holidays or ration annuity delivery days. He spent thirty-seven years at Wakpala but rarely saw any of his close relatives because of church jealousy and competition. As older relatives in Mad Bear's camp died, they sometimes mentioned Philip in their will. He inherited some land on that reservation, although he was actually enrolled and allotted at Yankton.

In 1888 he married my grandmother, Mary Sully Bordeaux. She had a background almost as strange as Philip's. In 1857 Alfred Sully, then a captain in the regular Army, was assigned to Fort Pierre for the winter. A lusty Irish bachelor, Sully lost no time in taking an Indian wife for his time on the frontier. Sully chose a young Yankton girl named Pehandutawin. By mid-1858 she bore him a daughter, my grandmother Akicitawin—"Soldier woman." A biography of Sully, written by Langdon Sully, his grandson, conveniently omitted Sully's dalliance with Pehandutawin, although he chose to reproduce a painting Sully had done of her and another Sioux girl, with the enigmatic comment that Sully's later white wife refused to allow him to hang the portrait in their home.

It is an ironic twist of fate that before the Civil War, when Sully was at Fort Randall across from the Yankton Reservation, his chief protagonist among the Yanktons was Saswe. Who could have predicted that their children would one day marry? While the Sully descendants refused to include an Indian in their family tree, many of my relatives thought it was nice to have Sully sneaking into our genealogical charts. Personally, I have never felt it was much of an honor. My aunt Ella, however, had several prints of the paintings of Thomas Sully, Alfred's famous artistic brother, and she always talked as if we had somehow inherited the Sully talent for painting—which of course none of us had.

Mary Sully had already experienced tragedy in her life. She had married a prosperous mixed-blood rancher named John Bordeaux and they had a nice ranch on what is now the Rosebud Reservation. They had two daughters, Annie and Rose. One day John took his family to Valentine, Nebraska, where he sold some cattle. They went into the hotel dining room to celebrate their first big success in the ranching business. While they were eating, some drunken cowboys came out of a saloon down the street and began shooting their pistols indiscriminately at signs and windows. A stray shot went through the window of the hotel dining room and killed John Bordeau. In an instant, Mary was widowed with two small daughters and little else. The money went to bury John.

Mary's mother, Pehandutawin, had taken the name Susan and married Peter LeGrand. Le Grand was a headman of the Half-Breed Band and represented Philip when he was unable to attend council meetings because of church business. So Philip and Mary had known each other since childhood. They were soon considering marriage since both needed a spouse to assist with the raising of their children. They were married within the year, and my aunt Ella was born in 1889.

Philip was now starting to have an impact on the mission work of the Episcopal Church. He learned to read English fairly well and studied Shakespeare on his own to improve his phrasing. A number of inspirational books had been translated into Dakota and he had copies of nearly every one of them. He read both English and Dakota versions to see how words and concepts should be translated. He would devote the whole of Saturday afternoon to preparing his sermons by going to an isolated spot, lying down, and watching the cloud formations passing by. Relying on

Saswe's wisdom, Tipi Sapa thought that by intensely study-ing the formation and dissolution of clouds, he could train himself to give sermons with a particular cadence and could determine how to create complete thoughts within one set of phrases. He became an outstanding preacher and orator and was called the Phillips Brooks of the Indian race by people in the East who had heard both men speak.

In 1892 Bishop Hare raised money to build a boarding and day school at St. Elizabeth's for the many Episcopalians who now belonged to the church in the southern part of the reservation. My grandfather was appointed to report on the progress of the school, which was operated by a devout white churchwoman from the Tuxedo, New York, area named Miss Francis. Thus, beginning in 1892, Philip's name appears occa-sionally in the annual reports of the commissioner of Indian Affairs describing the progress of the school at Oak Creek.

Under the treaty of 1868, the Teton Sioux had reserved a large portion of Wyoming and the western part of South Dakota from the Missouri River to the Black Hills. In 1877 the government confiscated the Black Hills and a portion of land between the forks of the Cheyenne River. The Yanktons were not involved in any of those transactions since their 1858 treaty had guaranteed the reservation along the Missouri. In 1888 the government decided to demand more land cessions and an allotment of the Teton Sioux lands in an effort to open South Dakota to settlement.

After failing to get the required three-fourths approval of the land cession in 1888, General George Crook was sent out to intimidate the Sioux and get them to agree to the cession. Visiting each reservation with an impressive force of soldiers, Crook obtained close to the required number of signatures, and the 1889 agreement was declared to be legal. This land cession had barely been approved before white settlers in

Brulé Teton leaders attending the council of the Sioux Land Commission, headed by General Crook. The Rosebud Reservation, May 1889. Nebraska State Historical Society, no. A547: 1-1.

eastern South Dakota began to agitate for the government to make the Yanktons cede part of their reservation for settlement. In 1891 and 1892 a commission was sent out to deal with the Yanktons. The government did its preliminary work very efficiently. Before the commission arrived, a small group of Indian men were secretly encouraged to begin agitating for money to pay bills and buy things. So it appeared as if the commission was responding to their pleas and was willing to do the tribe a favor by buying their land.

At issue was more than a land cession, however. The Yankton chiefs saw the meetings of the commission as an opportunity to renegotiate the treaties of 1837, in which they had ceded large parts of Iowa for a pittance, and 1858, when they had ceded parts of eastern South Dakota for even less. And they sought clarification of the ownership of the sacred Pipestone Quarry, which had been mistakenly declared to belong to the Sissetons and Wahpetons in an earlier treaty to which the Yanktons were not a party.

Here the irony of federal Indian policy can be seen. After the Yanktons agreed to the establishment of the reservation in 1858, Indian agents stepped into the traditional Yankton political processes. They insisted on sending certificates and medals to the men who headed the various bands and family groups, certifying that they were "chiefs" and implying that they held office by virtue of Bureau of Indian Affairs recognition.

When it came time to discuss the cession of lands in 1892, however, the government insisted that only a simple majority vote of the adult men was needed to approve it— since it was evident that most of the chiefs were dead set against ceding the lands. Tipi Sapa was very strongly opposed to the sale of lands, but church business kept him busy at Standing Rock and he could not attend some of the sessions.

A group of Dakota Indian catechists, 1895. Catechists were lay people or novices who could hold services when the missionary priest was not available. They were given these clothes by the bishop as part of their compensation for church work. Author's collection.

The government even held a feast during the negotiations and toasted Philip in his absence, more probably toasting the absence of his strong voice of opposition. We have always wondered if Bishop Hare did not create the church business that kept Philip from the meetings, since the bishop was a strong advocate of allotment and its role in breaking the power of the family in Indian political matters.

Mary and Philip had a son, Philip Ulysses, in 1893 and another daughter, Susan Mabel, in 1896. As the centuries changed, Philip suffered almost wholesale loss of his older relatives. His aunt Julia, Saswe's sister, died in 1897; his mother died in 1899; Dennis Grey Horn, his cousin and Julia's son, died in 1895; his sister Alice died in 1898; his sister Anna died in 1900; his sister Carrie died in 1901; and a nephew, George, died in 1899. With the loss of eight close relatives, all of them living at the White Swan community on the Yankton Reservation, Philip seemed to be constantly on the road returning to Yankton to hold family funerals. Most of these relatives had lived long lives and been living reminders of the days of freedom and of Saswe's vision. Because of them, Philip began to see his black clerical clothes and vestments as a modernized expression of the black tipi that Saswe had visited to receive his powers.

In 1900 my grandmother had an experience that nearly shattered the family. She dreamed that she was sitting on the front porch of the rectory and looked down the road to the west in front of the church, which was due west of the rectory in a row typical of the mission stations of those days. Suddenly she saw a small boy about two years old running down the road in the staggering gait that infants have. He was dressed in a light gray suit and had golden hair that came down almost to his shoulders. He was singing an incoherent baby song at the top of his lungs. Mary turned to look at her other children who were sitting on the porch. She said: "Oh, I think you're going to have a little brother."

As she looked at Philip Ulysses in joy, she saw his face fade away into a blur and in horror she realized that he would die and be replaced by the boy who was coming. Her other children learned of the dream and took every precaution to protect young Philip Ulysses. Philip and Mary tried their best to dismiss the dream as a temporary hallucination, but a pall had settled over the family. Mary shortly thereafter discovered that she was pregnant again. My father, Vine Deloria, was born in October 1901.

Philip Ulysses seemed to fade away with a disease that simply took the weight, color, and energy away from him. No one knew what ailed him and neither white nor Indian doctors could halt his decline. He died in August 1902. About a year later after the Easter service, Mary was standing on the porch of the rectory waiting for the women to come so they could begin to serve lunch. My father had been with his father greeting people at the church door when he decided to go home. So Mary saw my father, in the identical stumbling gait with a new gray suit on, coming down the road toward her—exactly as in her prophetic dream.

My grandfather had an almost fatal collapse as Philip Ulysses' illness worsened. Having lost two children and two wives, as well as most of his older relatives during the preceding six years, he went into a deep melancholy. He would drive into isolated places and do some of the ceremonies that Saswe had performed half a century before, but nothing seemed to work. He was inconsolable. At times friends would find him in some obscure clump of trees, exhausted and incoherent, and bring him back to the church. My aunts would later relive those days with such a fearful expression that they frightened everyone who heard their story. Philip

Reverend Philip Deloria, St. Elizabeth's Mission, Wakpala, South Dakota, 1906. Author's collection.

was a devout and hard-working Christian priest, but he could not reconcile the loss of this child with the promises of that religion. And he did not have Saswe's powers, which had brought Philip back from the grave as a child.

My father, as the sole surviving male, suffered from an overprotective atmosphere that developed in the family. My grandfather was almost fixated on him, and his sisters, both a good deal older than he, spent their time watching over him to keep him safe from any harm. My father, however, was determined to live the life of an ordinary reservation boy. He learned to rope and ride horses almost as soon as he could walk. He idolized Fred Lane, the man who had married his stepsister Lyma, and he wanted to become a cowboy like Fred. But my grandfather was determined that he would become a priest like himself. The motives were clear: Philip saw his black clerical clothes as a physical representation of the black tipi of Saswe. There were four purification tents and so there should be four generations of the family following a religious vocation.

By the early 1900s my grandfather had become a living symbol of the white Christian belief that Indians could make progress in civilization. The Episcopal Church had been unusually fortunate in having a number of Indian clergy who were brilliant orators, attractive to eastern white audiences, and very influential among their own people. Sherman Coolidge, an Arapaho, had been orphaned in the 1870s Indian wars, educated as a white, and ordained as a missionary to his own people at the Wind River Reservation in Wyoming. He was another Native priest who received great plaudits for his conversion. Tipi Sapa became a Mason and participated in their ritual, recognizing that these kinds of relationships were a big help in influencing white society to understand his people.

Among the Episcopalian Sioux at the time were three other outstanding Native clergy: Amos Ross, who had been rescued from the Fort Snelling stockade during the Minnesota war in 1862 by Bishop Whipple; Baptiste Lambert, a Yankton mixed-blood and chief of a band on the reservation; and Luke Walker, a Yanktonais who had been one of the first Sioux to be ordained a priest. These men and my grandfather made up the "Big Four" and were regarded by the Sioux Episcopalians as their most important spiritual leaders. All of these men were robust, standing over six feet, and the Sioux admired tall men. Each man had a family background of both political and religious leadership, and all of them could speak both English and Dakota fluently. It is said that these men always appeared together at church meetings, partially for protection from the many people who would be requesting favors and partly to emphasize to the bishop and other church officials that the Sioux people were united behind them.

With the death of Bishop Hare in 1908, the Episcopal church work began to change radically as new people took over the administration of programs. The House of Bishops, instead of choosing a Native clergyman to replace Bishop Hare, now elected a series of rather drab, barely competent bishops who only wanted to rise in the church hierarchy. The intellectual horizon of the time did not reach beyond Rudyard Kipling's view of "the white man's burden," and efforts to continue to advance Native men to the priesthood declined as energies went into recruiting seminary-trained white clergy.

The Indian work was segregated, and special attention was given to the needs of white clergy. Separate annual convocations of the churches were held. The excuse was that the Indian clergy did not understand enough about

Christianity to serve in a white parish. In reality the South Dakota whites had strong prejudices against Indians and did not want an Indian priest serving them. White clergy needed a living wage to work for the church in South Dakota. They usually were paid about twice as much as the Native clergy on the excuse that they were trained in a seminary and therefore better understood the deeper complexities of Christianity. Most of the Native clergy were paid so little that they had to sell their allotments to provide for their families. When they complained about their low wages, they were told that priests must make sacrifices to serve God. And the bishops argued that white clergy had given up comfortable parishes in the East to come to South Dakota to help the Sioux.

In 1911 Philip was invited to attend the organizing meeting of the Society of American Indians, the first national gathering of educated Indians who had achieved some success in the white man's world. Many famous Indians such as Charles Eastman, Carlos Montezuma, Thomas Sloan, and Arthur Hewitt attended the sessions. The group convened in Columbus, Ohio, on Columbus Day, a time and place having great symbolic meaning for the non-Indians who sponsored the gathering. The first national Indian organization didn't last very long. Quarrels over the role of the Bureau of Indian Affairs in Indian life, sparked by Carlos Montezuma's hatred of the Bureau, eventually caused its downfall. But Philip did make many new friends through the activities of the organization, and they often visited him at Standing Rock.

In 1915 Mary died of a liver disease after a long illness. My grandfather mourned for a long time over her loss, but was faced with the immediate problem of how to raise a teenaged son. His daughters were now either married or in college. Within a week of my grandmother's death, Philip contacted Bishop Beecher of Nebraska and arranged to have my father admitted to a diocesan school, Kearney Military Academy in Kearney, Nebraska. My father arrived by train a few days later, still in shock from the loss of his mother and unable to speak much English. Years later he would tell me that he lay awake for hours each night to make certain his roommates were asleep before crying for his mother and wondering about his fate. He attended Kearney for five years, mastering English and becoming the cadet major of the student body and an annual four-letter athlete in football, basketball, baseball, and track.

A problem facing the Yanktons served to distract Philip from his personal sorrow and helped him work through it. Soon after my grandmother's death, he became involved in the tribe's effort to resolve a dispute with the government. Beginning in 1837 there had been disputes between the government and several Sioux tribes and bands over the ownership of the Red Pipestone Quarry in Minnesota, where many tribes got their pipestone. The Yanktons were regarded as the guardians of this sacred location, but as the Sissetons and Wahpetons were drawn closer to the Sioux City–Yankton area by the fur trade, they became the closest Sioux groups to use the quarry. While attempting to clear western Minnesota of Indian claims, the government mistakenly identified these Sioux as the owners of the quarry.

In the 1858 treaty, when the Yanktons ceded large parts of eastern South Dakota and northwestern Iowa, they refused to sign the treaty unless the United States admitted that the quarry belonged to them and had never been ceded. This controversy continued over the years, and in the agreement of 1892 the subject came up again. This agreement contained the following article:

If the Government of the United States questions the ownership of the Pipestone Reservation
by the Yankton tribe of Sioux Indians, under the
treaty of April 19th, 1858, including the fee to the
land as well as the right to work the quarries, the
Secretary of the Interior shall as speedily as possible refer the matter to the Supreme Court of the
United States, to be decided by that tribunal. And
the United States shall furnish, without cost to the
Yankton Indians, at least one competent attorney
to represent the interests of the tribe before the
court. If the Secretary of the Interior shall not,
within one year after the ratification of this agreement by Congress, refer the question of the ownership of the said Pipestone Reservation to the
Supreme Court, as provided for above, such failure
upon his part shall be construed as, and shall be, a
waiver by the United States of all rights to the
ownership of the said Pipestone Reservation, and
the same shall thereafter be solely the property of
the Yankton tribe of the Sioux Indians, including
the fee to the land. (28 Stat 314, Article XVI)

To avoid the eventuality of forfeit, since Congress could
not by agreement direct the Supreme Court to take the case,
federal representatives were sent again to the Yanktons in
1899 to offer them an immense sum of money to cede the
quarry to the United States. But the agreement was never
ratified. The Yanktons then began a tedious process of lob-
bying to get compensation by statute. They sent a delegation
to Washington to every Congress until 1928 to plead for just
compensation for the loss of their sacred quarry. Continuing
to be chief of Band Eight, Philip was a member of most of

Dakota priests at St. Elizabeth's Mission, Sakpala, 1922. From left to right three of the "Big Four": Luke Walker, Philip Deloria, and Baptiste Lambert. Author's collection.

these delegations. In 1926 hearings were held in Lake Andes, a small town on the Yankton Reservation, and in 1927 at the Pipestone Quarry itself in Minnesota. My father was one of the translators during those hearings. Through the legal expertise of Jennings Wise, a former attorney general of the United States, a bill was finally passed and the Yanktons received $100,000 and kept the right to gather materials at the quarry.

My grandfather, who had remained a chief during this time, was appointed a member of the business committee to solve the problem. Along with other elders, he went to Washington several times and attended the meetings held at Lake Andes and Pipestone. His health was failing, and photographs taken at the time show him as a frail old man, doing his duty but aware that this would be his last effort on behalf of his people. But this community work, to which he devoted much energy, helped him adjust to the loss of his wife and the scattering of his family.

After my father graduated from Kearney Military Academy, Philip was able to get him a scholarship to St. Stephen's College in Annandale, New York, a small Episcopal college originally established to train men for the Episcopal priesthood. It was failing to perform this task primarily because most eligible young Episcopalians were headed for Wall Street, not the sanctuary. St. Stephen's then sought to duplicate the success of Notre Dame and Fordham and become a football power to attract students and ensure national church support. St. Stephen's was eager to enroll my father, whose athletic reputation had been firmly established at Kearney. My father therefore got a good scholarship to go to college. He was terribly naive about his status.

When I was ready to go to college, he told me not to worry, that missionaries' sons received full scholarships and

Witnesses and attorneys for the Red Pipestone Quarry land claim, County Courthouse, Lake Andes, South Dakota, 1926. Philip Deloria, front row, second from left; Baptiste Lambert, second from right. Author's collection.

interested churchmen came and bought you clothes and took you out to dinner. It was difficult for me to convince him that he had been a semi-pro athlete in the hypocritical world of college football. In his second year at St. Stephen's, my father threw a fifty-five-yard pass, earning him honorable mention by Walter Camp in his annual All-American listing and giving him the collegiate record for longest pass, tied coincidentally with another Indian, John Levi of Haskell Institute, a government boarding school in Kansas. In those days the forward pass was measured by "distance in the air" and not by the yardage made by the receiver after the catch. It always amazed me that he could throw one of those old balls that distance.

Philip retired from church work in 1925, while my father was still in college. He wanted to get a small house in Wakpala and live out his days among his friends and relatives on the Standing Rock Reservation. But the bishop pressured him to return to White Swan on the Yankton Reservation, contending that he would be returning to his people. The bishop was afraid the new priest would not be received well by the people if Tipi Sapa lived in the vicinity. Philip argued that he had served at Standing Rock for almost four decades and his old friends were all at Wakpala, while all his close relatives and friends at Yankton had died. But the bishop was adamant.

Obediently Philip agreed, and the church built a small house for him at White Swan and he was put in charge of St. Philip's Chapel there. He quickly became lonely for his old friends at Standing Rock, and his letters to the bishop asking if he could return are heartbreaking. In retrospect it seems as if Philip didn't want to be at White Swan because it brought back the hardships and tragedies of his life. His father was buried at the agency at Greenwood, his wooden

Further hearings on the Red Pipestone Quarry land claim, Pipestone Minnesota, September 30, 1927. Philip Deloria is standing in the fifth row from the bottom, on the left. National Archives.

grave marker now faded away. His three previous wives and deceased children, with the exception of Philip Ulysses, were buried at White Swan, together with his sisters and their families. He married again after my grandmother died to escape the loneliness of an empty house. His fourth wife, Julia, took good care of him. To hold the Sunday services at White Swan, however, Philip had to walk by the graveyard that contained all the shattered dreams of his life.

Although Tipi Sapa still believed that accommodation to the white man's way, including his religion, offered the best hope for his people to survive, he also began to speak out bluntly in favor of the old ways. "Nobody has any fun anymore," he is reported to have said, "Everything is so serious and we don't have time to visit." He did fill his days with visiting, however, and my cousin Philip Lane, who had been orphaned in 1926 with the death of his mother Lyma Rose, came to live with him, bringing immeasurable cheer to the old man.

Young Philip spent a few days in the classroom and then stopped going to school so he could stay home with his grandfather. Our aunt Ella, who was making her way in college, was horrified when she learned of Phil's absence and told Tipi Sapa that Philip should be in school. But my grandfather said that Philip could learn more from him, and he refused to let the boy go to school. Phil Lane has a storehouse of memories of these years, one of which captures the life of the old men at Yankton.

Phil said that every so often grandfather would tell him to hitch up the team and take him visiting. They would travel many miles until they reached the home of one of the old men. There the people would be ready and waiting. Usually four of these old men would gather. They would be given nice rocking chairs under a shady tree and they would visit.

This scene sounds like an idyllic reunion of old men, but it has a strange dimension.

Phil said that one day he realized that these men were not talking out loud. They would sit, casually smoke their pipes, and lean back in intense concentration with their eyes closed. A long silence would then prevail. After five or ten minutes, one of them would suddenly lean forward, open his eyes and make comments on some subject, emphasizing part of a story that had not been told out loud. The others would comment and perhaps say a few words, and then the four would again relapse into silence.

It was when the old men came to visit at the church rectory that Phil Lane said he began to ask questions. One day my grandfather called Phil and told him he was expecting a visit. By mid-afternoon the old men and their families were spotted on the horizon headed for the rectory. Phil wanted to know how these old men had agreed to gather together. No one had come to their home between visits to see if another visit was scheduled or whose home they would visit. In fact, Phil said, there had been no communication at all. Whatever it was that these men were doing, they were telepathically connected to each other. Phil said that the older our grandfather got, the more powers he seemed to display.

Philip began having strokes that greatly hampered his ability to speak and walk. He went to the white doctors in Lake Andes. Soon realizing it was beyond his ability to pay for this medical care, he began seeing the traditional Indian healers on the reservation. At Ella's urging, Tipi Sapa had purchased an automobile, and it was Phil's task to drive the old man to the healers. After helping Tipi Sapa into the car, Phil would pile several pillows on the driver's seat so that he could see the road well enough to drive. When they went to have Tipi Sapa healed, with young Phil hardly visible behind the wheel and Philip and Julia in plain sight in the back seat, it would seem as if the car was driving itself. The traditional healers spent a lot of time with Philip, who seemed to be subject to a continuing series of small strokes, and kept him alive through some terribly difficult times.

My father graduated from St. Stephens in 1926 and returned home. After his successful college career as a football player, he hoped to get a job as a coach at one of the Indian schools. He spent a year as boy's athletic advisor at Chilocco, but the job was not renewed. He returned home to find that Philip was determined that he go to seminary and become a priest. Wanting to avoid entering the priesthood, my father got a job in a coal mine near Colorado Springs and worked a year as a miner. When he returned, he saw that Philip was very sick and might not live much longer. In the most urgent terms he could, the old man prevailed upon my father to go to seminary.

My father often told me how difficult it was for him to give in to his father's wishes. He said that his motives were not the best as he headed for the seminary in New York in the fall of 1928. He figured that his father could not live much longer, and to please him he would stay in seminary as long as Philip lived. Then he would leave and hope to take up ranching at Standing Rock or coaching, if he could get a job.

In the summer of 1927 when the news broke that President Calvin Coolidge was going to visit the Black Hills, Philip, Amos Ross, and Baptiste Lambert wrote the president to invite him to attend the Niobrara Convocation and see the condition of the Sioux, who were living in pitiful poverty and close to starvation. Coolidge did come to the convocation, which was held at Pine Ridge, more likely wishing to endear himself to the bishop than to see what was happening to the Sioux. When he arrived, the people gathered for a panoramic photograph with the clergy and the president. Coolidge immediately got back into his car and returned to the Black Hills. Old timers have told me that the visit was less than three minutes and that Coolidge did not even look back and wave as his car sped away. Nevertheless, the three old priests wrote a glowing letter to Coolidge thanking him for his time, and it was prominently published in one of the church magazines.

It now became a contest of wills between my father and his father. Philip was almost totally incapacitated. The family moved to Mission, South Dakota, near Julia's family. My aunts were furious because they wanted my grandfather to continue to live at White Swan. My father threw himself into seminary studies and in the summertime worked in a boy's camp in the Catskills with urban youth recruited by one of the New York City churches. He and my grandfather exchanged a few formal, businesslike letters; Philip did not express much affection or encouragement to my father.

The three years of seminary passed and my father was ready to graduate when word reached him that Philip had had a massive stroke. This time it appeared he could not survive. My father rushed back to South Dakota and took his new clericals to wear when he saw his father. His graduation was still a month away, but the seminary officials told him he could tell his father that he was now graduated and ready to be ordained a deacon in the church. My father arrived in Mission, put on his new clothes, and went into the room to see his father. Tears flooded out any conversation the two might have had; they just shook hands and comforted each other. My father said that he felt committed to being a priest when he saw how happy his father was. A third generation had now entered the Black Tipi. Two days later, Philip Deloria, Tipi Sapa, peacefully passed away.

The Brotherhood of Christian Unity, which Philip had helped to found, provided a large but simple gravestone for him in the Mission cemetery. At the Niobrara Convocation that year, the people decided to remember Tipi Sapa by always having "Guide Me, O Thou Great Jehovah" as the closing hymn of the gathering. I was born two years later, and I remember how kind everyone was to me as a little toddler when people would say, "That's Tipi Sapa's grandson." I could never understand why singing that hymn brought tears to so many people's eyes as the convocation closed.

In 1936 when they were completing the National Cathedral in Washington, D.C., in the reredos of the building were placed sixty statutes entitled "The Company of Heaven." The statues included apostles, saints, and more recent heroes of the faith. Tipi Sapa was one of three Americans whose statues were included, along with the current dean of the cathedral and Phillips Brooks, the great New England preacher. Sadly, none of the family were invited to attend the unveiling of the statue. But postcards and posters were made of the statue to be used in church fundraising efforts.

My father was ordained as a deacon and then as a priest. His great speeches in the winter of 1940 made him the national symbol of Episcopal mission work. He was the first Indian to be appointed to direct a national church denomination's Indian mission work. But when he tried to move the Episcopal Church to support the tribes during the termination era, he lost the church's support and was forced to resign after four years at the post. He had to seek a parish once again. In 1961 he was made archdeacon of the Episcopal work in South Dakota. He served the remainder of his life

until retirement traveling that state trying to keep the
church work going. But time and a series of lethargic bishops
had reduced the work to a shadow of what it had been sev-
enty-five years before. The remaining church schools had
been closed, there was no recruitment of Native clergy, and
people had moved away from the many small chapels that
once dotted the reservation landscape.

      *   *   *   *

Many people still have pictures of the Big Four taken at
the Niobrara Convocation in 1926 at Lower Brulé, when
these men were still in their physical prime, standing tall in
their priestly garb with dignified expressions on their faces.
A number of people have sent me a copy of the photo, asking if I have ever seen it, and tracing out my blood relationship with them. Philip was said to have converted many of
the Sioux to Christianity. By 1900 there were more than
12,000 Sioux belonging to the Episcopal Church. In view of
Philip's continuing work as a chief of Band Eight and his
interest in renewing the old ways after his retirement, it
seems to me that, like his father, he saw Christianity as the
only viable alternative for his people in those early reservation days. Saswe had directed him down the road just as
Philip later got my father to travel the same road. They created a family heritage that has been a heavy burden but one
that seemingly could not have been avoided once Saswe
chose the red road.

On July 19th, 1989, I was sitting with my father in the
dry desert heat in the patio of Our Place, a supervised care
home in Tucson, Arizona. My father, then a frail eighty-
seven years old, had to live in this sterile environment
because earlier that year his Alzheimer's condition had

The Big Four (left to right): Baptiste Lambert, Luke Walker, Philip Deloria, and Amos Ross. The Niobrara Convocation, 1926, Lower Brulé. Author's collection.

grown much worse. He no longer recognized my mother, and his mind often drifted back to his childhood on the Standing Rock Reservation. He often did not recognize me, but on this occasion he seemed to have reasonably clear periods. We were able to talk, although our conversation was punctuated with long silences. He was sad, quite weary, and did not like the patio area but seemed resigned to it.

I was particularly eager to talk that day because it was the fiftieth anniversary of a day when his life radically changed from that of an ordinary missionary priest to the continuing path that our family had walked for a century and a half. On July 19, 1939, Martin, South Dakota, where he was rector of All Saints Church, was hit by a devastating tornado. It destroyed the local Chevrolet garage, ruined the movie theatre, and picked up his little Episcopal Church and rolled it into the street, taking most of the rectory roof off and distributing it around town.

The following day, as my father was surveying the ruins, Cliff Cowan, an old friend from Ohio, drove through Martin and stopped to see the damage. He and my father walked around the littered churchyard. Cowan said, "I'll be in touch with you before Christmas," and drove off to see the Black Hills. Shortly before Christmas, my father received a letter from Cliff saying that he had arranged a speaking tour of the Episcopal Diocese of Ohio so my father could raise funds to build another church.

In January my father went east and told the story of the great storm, the church's missions to the people of the Pine Ridge Reservation, and the story of the Sioux people. He raised a good deal of money, and the cathedral of St. John in Denver made up the rest of the funds. A nice new church and rectory were built in Martin. Through this trip my father emerged from the role of an obscure priest hidden in the grasslands of South Dakota to become a nationally promi-nent church leader.

I was overly anxious to hear what my father would say when remembering that day, and I brought up the subject over and over the whole afternoon. His eyes got misty but he either did not recall the tornado or wanted not to remember it, although he had told the story hundreds of times before. He finally looked skyward and held his gaze for several moments, finally commenting softly, "I don't deserve this. I did everything you wanted."

About three weeks later, my cousin, Phil Lane, came to see my father. They spent several days talking Dakota, laughing at old memories, and enjoying each other. On the last day, as Phil was leaving, my father followed him to the gate, and shook his hand briefly. As Phil turned to go through the gate, my father said in a soft, plaintive voice, "Let's go home, Bish." Bish was his nickname for my cousin, given in happier days when Phil was just a youngster at Wakpala, South Dakota.

My father then just seemed to fade away. He died about six months later.

Indian priests of Niobrara Deaconcy of the Sioux Indian Episcopal Church. Crow Creek Mission, Fort Thompson, South Dakota, 1926. Philip Deloria is seated in the first row, fifth from the right, a large hat coveing part of his face. Author's collection.

Crow Buttes, South Dakota. Photo © by Philip J. Deloria.

PART II:
The People of Tipi Sapa

BY SARAH OLDEN

Working on the winter count, the record of events of the past year.
Nebraska State Historical Society, no. A547: 2-1.

The Origin of the Indians

According to Indian tradition, in the old days all the Indian peoples crossed some great river; but whence they came originally, they cannot say. It was their custom to travel in the nighttime, and they wandered at random over wild, unknown lands. In the early dawn they were able "to see the nakedness of the land," the countless hills and valleys, fertile plains, the lakes, creeks, winding rivers, and beautiful timber. They then spied out ways over which they could have traveled far better if they had only known of them at the time, but they had been able to perceive nothing under cover of night.

They wandered from the West—the Darkening Land— toward the Sunrise. Some were able to reach the Big Water in the Sunrise (the Atlantic Ocean). One tribe, the Cheyenne, strayed into the country now named Minnesota. The Cheyenne are now found only in Montana [and Oklahoma].

The Indians are a very old people. They lived in tents, journeyed from place to place, as did the nomadic tribes of the Orient, and camped wherever they found water and good pasture for their horses. In war, they thought it most important to take from the enemy as many horses as possible. They traded, bought, and sold with horses as we do with money. Even now, they often pay their debts, among themselves and to the white man, with horses.

In reckoning time, the Indians counted from sunrise to sunrise as a day and three hundred and sixty-five days as a year. Some of them noted the occurrence of an extra day occasionally. They talked about it a great deal, but were never of one mind on the subject. Some maintained that every few years the extra day occurred. The record of the days in a year was kept by carving notches on thick sticks of wood.

From the earliest times, the Indians believed in a Supreme Being who ruled the universe. They prayed to visible objects, especially the sun, moon, and stars; and they reverenced even the trees and the rocks. They did not actually worship the objects themselves, but looked upon them as instruments of power through which their prayers reached the Great Spirit.

The religious code of the Sioux Indians, the tribe treated in this book, was similar, in many respects, to the Ten Commandments. The Above, the Supreme Being, the Mysterious One, "Wakantanka," was held in awe and veneration. He was all-powerful. He could give them whatever they wanted if they were good, and could keep them from getting anything they desired if they were bad. Children were expected to honor and obey their parents and help them in every way possible. All the young people had to observe the precepts and teachings of the old men, the chiefs, and leaders. In them was vested the civil authority. The people were to use no deceit; they were to hurt nobody by word or deed. Lying and slandering were disreputable. We shall see, further on, the evil effects of gossip upon girls and women, including even suicide. The untruthful and the backbiters were held in no respect whatever. The people were urged on almost every occasion to care for the poor, the weak, and the little ones; and generosity and kindness were always highly commended.

Murder in one's own Circle was considered a terrible crime and deserving of death. Stealing, except in war or in certain kinds of ceremony and play, was disgraceful. To covet and go off with another man's wife was a great evil and, as will be shown later, one worthy of severe punishment for both offenders. The men and the women acted the parts in life that they considered to be allotted to them. The bearing of burdens seemed to be shared by both sexes to an almost equal degree.

The Dakota Nation was divided into twelve bands: the Cheyenne River, Crow Creek, Devil's Lake, Flandreau, Lower Brulé, Pine Ridge, Poplar, Rosebud, Santee, Sisseton, Standing Rock, and Yankton. [This listing is of course incorrect since Miss Olden could not grasp the idea that the bands of Sioux found on reservations in those days were not the original groupings. This is actually a list of the Sioux reservations in North and South Dakota. I have left this statement in the text to show that already by 1918, the old band designations had given way to reservation identities in the minds of many people.]

Long ago, there was another division of the Sioux called the Sans Arcs, who preserved the beautiful legend of the Pipe. This Pipe, in use from the earliest times, occupied a position of peculiar importance and was held in the deepest reverence. It was entrusted to the care of a highly honored man and was brought out and smoked with much ceremony on great and solemn occasions.

THE PIPE STORY

Years ago, within the Dakota Nation, there was a band known as the Sans Arcs [Itazipco]. Out of this band of Indians, two especially favored and handsome young men were, on one occasion, selected and commissioned to ride out and find where the buffalo were. While these young men were riding in the wild country, bent on their mission of finding the buffalo, they saw someone in the distance walking toward them.

As always, they were on the alert lest some enemy should surprise them and take their scalps. The most natural thing for them to do was to hide in the bushes. There they sat and waited for the figure to come in sight. Finally, up the slope it came. It proved to be a Beautiful Woman. At a distance she halted and looked toward them in their hiding place, and they knew that she could see them. On her left arm she carried what looked like a stick, bundled up in bunches of sagebrush. She was fair to look upon.

One of the men said to his companion: "I covet her. She is lovely beyond anyone I ever saw. She shall be mine."

The other said, "How can you dare to entertain such thoughts when she is so wondrously beautiful and holy, so far above our race?"

The woman, standing over in the distance, heard them and laid down her bundle. "Come," she said. "What is it you wish?" And the first man went to her and laid hands on her, as though to claim her, when from somewhere above came a whirlwind, and after it, a mist. The mist enveloped the man and the Beautiful Woman, then cleared away, leaving the Woman standing with the bundle on her left arm, and the man, now a heap of bones, at her feet.

The companion, who stood rapt in wonder and awe, was now addressed by the Beautiful Woman. She said: "I am making this journey to your tribe, the Sans Arcs. Among your people there lives a good man. His name is Tatanka Woslal Mani (Bull Walking Upright). To him especially I am come. Go home and tell your tribe I am on my way. Have them

Ceremonial lodge. Nebraska State Historical Society, no. A547: 2-96.

move camp and pitch their tents in a circle, leaving an opening toward the north. In the center of the circle, opposite the opening, they are to erect a large tipi, also facing the north. There I will meet Tatanka Woslal Mani and his people."

[After all the preparations had been made, the woman entered the camp, sat down, and began teaching the people.] To Tatanka Woslal Mani she gave the gift she carried. Taking away the sage branches it was wrapped in, she revealed a small pipe made of red pipestone. This type of stone later was universally used for Indian pipes. On the pipe was carved, most ingeniously, a tiny little outline of a calf; hence the name "Calf Pipe," which is sometimes applied to the original Pipe.

With the Pipe, the Beautiful Woman gave them a code of morals by which they were to live with one another in the tribe. Moreover, she gave them forms of prayers to be said when invoking the "One Above." When they prayed to Him, they were to use the Pipe in the ceremony. When they were hungry, they were instructed to undo the Pipe and lay it bare to the air. Then the buffalo would come near, to a place where the men could easily hunt and kill them; and the children, women, and men would have food and be happy.

In the lesson that the tribe received on that day, everything was good and true. In observing the moral code just received, they knew they would be happy. By invoking the aid of the Strong One above and using the Pipe in the ceremony, they would be certain of receiving the blessings asked. The Woman completed her message, turned, and departed. Slowly she walked away while all the tribe watched in awe. Outside the doorway of the circle she stopped for an instant, lay down on the ground, and rose again in the form of a beautiful black buffalo cow. Again she lay down, this time to arise in the form of a red buffalo cow! A third time she lay down and arose a brown buffalo cow! The fourth and last time, she appeared as a spotless white buffalo cow. In this form she turned to the north and walked into the distance, finally vanishing over the hill.

During her strange visit, the Beautiful Woman instructed the people how to decorate their bodies when they were happy. The earth, she said, was their mother, for the earth nursed them and cared for them. Hence, when they wanted to honor her, they were to decorate themselves as their mother did, in black and red and brown and white, the colors the buffalo cow assumed in her different appearances. The earth dressed herself in white, for did not the people find white earth in certain places? (Gray clay.) Was she not somewhere clad in red (Vermillion, South Dakota), and in brown, as the brown earth on the hillsides? The black earth, found in the badlands of South Dakota, was well known to the Indians, who used it as paint and dye. They were authorized to use these colors when they painted themselves for festive occasions. But when any of the people had done wrong or had taken human life in the tribe, they were wrong in the sight of the Great Spirit and had to cover themselves with common mud. Hence arose the custom for a murderer to cover his body with ordinary dirt and clay. For many years these four colors—white, black, red, and brown—were the only ones in use among the Indians.

Tatanka Woslal Mani taught his people the many good things the Beautiful Woman taught him. Always carefully wrapped and laid away was the sacred Pipe she brought them, the Calf Pipe. Fashioned after it were other pipes used in different sorts of Indian ceremonies. The legend runs that Tatanka Woslal Mani had the Pipe until he was over one hundred years old. Every little while he called the people together, untied the bundle, and communicated the lessons that had been taught to him. When he grew feeble, he made a great feast and handed over the Pipe and the lessons to Wihinapa (Sunrise), a worthy man who used the Pipe in the same way and passed it on, before his death, to one Pehin Sapa (Black Hair) with instructions to use it in the same manner.

Pehin Sapa gave it to Hehaka Pa (Elk's Head) who, at his death, left it to Mato Nakpa (Bear's Ear). Tatanka Ptesan (White Buffalo Bull) was the next to receive it. After him, Herlogeca (Hollow Horn) was the custodian; and in recent times [around 1900] Hollow Horn gave the Pipe to Hehaka Pa (Elk's Head) the Second, who died a few years ago [around 1910], leaving the Pipe and its teachings to his daughter, whose husband is Zuya Śica. Hehaka Pa had a son, but preferred to give the pipe to his daughter, because his son had married a Standing Rock woman and had left the Sans Arcs band. It was this son, who came from the western part of the Cheyenne [River] Reservation, where the Sans Arcs are located, who told this story to Tipi Sapa. He remained to dine with Tipi Sapa and his family.

[Some additional information was passed down in the full version of Tipi Sapa's account that Miss Olden did not record. He said that before White Buffalo Calf Woman would come into the camp circle, the people were told to destroy all their weapons. The people burned their bows and arrows and were utterly helpless should an enemy have approached them. As a result of this requirement, they were thereafter called "Sans Arcs"—Itazipco—those without bows, and their role among the Teton Sioux was that of peacemaker.]

The Circle

The Circle was the emblem of eternity [for the Sioux. They always camped in a circle for protection against their enemies and so that they could remember that they were all equals. If there were enough tipis to form a circle, it would be used as a protective and religious arrangement for making a camp.] The middle tent, or large tipi in the center of the Circle was a sacred place. The ground was leveled, and braided sweetgrass was laid upon it. The end opposite the door was held in as much regard as the chancel of a church. On solemn occasions, one of the chosen men in the Circle occupied this place of honor and conducted ceremonies with the pipe. Taking it in his hands, he pointed it to heaven, to the four corners of the winds, and to the earth and prayed, saying, "Great Spirit (or Great Father), send me the Spirit of the buffalo" (or any other spirit he desired).

After smoking the pipe, he said to those present, "These prayers of mine will be carried in this smoke to the Supreme Being (or Creator)." If any bad people, such as liars and murderers or dishonorable or unclean persons (that is, those who had gone off with the wives of other men) came near the middle tent, they were driven away at once. If they should enter that sacred place, it was feared they might drive away the spirit of the buffalo, as they themselves were possessed of evil spirits. Such characters had to wear mourning and wander about outside of the Circle.

In the Circle, certain traditions called "old men's instructions" were used to teach girls as well as boys. The old men were obliged to prove themselves worthy of handing on traditions in accordance with those who came before them. A young man was taught to be loyal to the Supreme Being and to his Circle. He was never to tell any secrets or to disclose any weaknesses of his Circle. He was obliged to prepare himself constantly for two forms of action—hunting and fighting. Above all else, he was to be brave and to kill, if possible, four men from among the enemy. He would then be given four feathers as marks of distinction. These feathers were to be worn pointing in different directions in the hair at the top of his braid.

The man who first took aim and killed one of the approaching enemy did not receive a feather. It was given to the one who went forward and hit him after he was down. This required greater bravery because it was done in the face of the enemy and if not managed quickly and skillfully, it exposed the attacker to capture and a terrible death. The feather received for performing the first such act was worn straight upward; the second feather was worn sloping; the third, at a sharper angle; and the fourth, flat (horizontal). For any such exploit in which the man was wounded, he received a red feather.

When a warrior had won four feathers and had acted according to "the old men's instructions," he would be chosen by the vote of the old men to become a "leader" and would hold that title for some years. During that time he had the care of some of the poor and the orphans in his Circle. There were several leaders in the Circle. They were expected to have

Nebraska State Historical Society, no. A547: 2-143.

many horses taken from the enemy, as well as one or more scalps. In fighting, the Indians took the scalps of their enemies, very often when their victims were yet alive. If it was done skillfully with a sharp knife, the scalp peeled from the head like the skin from a banana. It was soaked in water for some time, scraped carefully inside, and dried thoroughly. It was then painted red inside and well oiled to make it soft. Scalps with long hair were of great value and highly respected.

The man who had taken a scalp carried it home with great pride and gave it to his sister, if he had one. She was very proud of it too and carried it with her at the next dance she attended. The scalp was kept in the family. During times of warfare, it was attached to the lower part of the bridle of the horse ridden in the fight, the ghastly hair waving about as the horse ran. This trophy showed the enemy that its owner could kill and take scalps and that therefore he was to be greatly feared.

After they returned from fighting and were in the Circle once more, the leaders were honored. They placed the feathers they had won in their hair according to the proper mode of wearing them. They then took off their clothing and rubbed their bodies all over with the soft fat obtained from around the tail of a buffalo mixed with soot from charred wood. Those who received straight feathers (*Tona wiyaka owotanna aopaȥanpi kin on*) sang this song:

SONG

Why have I done this?
Because I want the right to wear a feather
Why have I done this?
Because I have not, as yet, the right to wear
Black paint on my body

ODOWAN KIN
Toka e un hecamon he?
Aopazan manica e on
Toka e un hecamon he?
Itisabya manica e on

A man in the Circle might go forward to take the clothing and weapons laid aside by one of these brave men and
succeed in getting everything away from him, since these
things would now bring good luck. A number of young girls
jumped on horses, rode about, and joined in the singing.
After going around the Circle once, the leaders broke away
and went to their own tipis. Soon they were brought out and
taken to a large tent that had been put up for them in the
middle of the Circle. This they were supposed to occupy for
four days.

A felled tree was set up in the middle of the Circle, its
bark removed and its trunk painted black. The scalps taken
during the fighting were hung upon it. The old chiefs would
announce that there must be a dance around the tree. The
young women prepared themselves by blackening their faces
and dressing themselves in soft, beautiful, buckskin gowns
worked with designs in colored beads and porcupine quills.
The wives, daughters, and sisters of the warriors represented
them in the dance and wore eagles' feathers with some of the
web stripped off. The feathers were colored red to signify the
wounds inflicted on the enemy and the flowing blood. The
bows, arrows, lances, spears, and any other weapons used in
fighting were carried aloft by the women in the dance as a
symbol of the bravery of the warriors.

During the dance while the weapons were being shown
off by the women, they sang (*Tohand wacipi conhan wipe kin
winyan kin deyapi eca*):

SONG (FOR THE WARRIORS)
The Above (Supreme Being) gave me this
(That is why) I have done this

ODOWAN KIN (WAKTE)
Iye (Wankata kin) de maqu
Heon (etanhan) deced ecamon

At this point the braves came from the large tent with
their feathers arranged in their hair. The man who had
acquired the clothing and weapons of one of the braves would
come forward and say that though he had been known heretofore by a certain name, he now intended, upon receiving his
first feather, to give it up and to assume a new one—Chasing
Bear, perhaps, or something of the kind. He then would call
some old woman forward and present her with a horse; next he
would give one to an orphan boy; and so on until he had given
away all the horses brought home by him from the enemy. He
would attempt to leave at this point, but the old men would
call him forward again on account of his good deeds. The
women danced holding aloft their weapons, and singing:

SONG
Somewhere a Crow (Indian) lies dead
Chasing Bear has done it
He is well named
He has done well!

ODOWAN KIN
Kangi (Wicaśa) hed wanke do e
Mato Wakuwa he econ we
He tanyan otaninye
He tanyan econ we!

This is equivalent to:

> Saul has killed his thousands,
> David his tens of thousands!

or

> Saul koktopawinge kte,
> David koktopawinge wikcemna!

These dances continued for two months after the warriors had returned. [This song was sung by the Hunkpapas and Blackfeet Sioux who fought against the Crow people. The Yanktons would have used the tribal designations of Pawnee, Omaha, or Ponca in their song.]

If a leader was defeated, when he came back he pierced his arms through with sticks, one for each man lost. With these sticking in his flesh, he went around the Circle crying. This showed his deep sorrow and repentance because the Great Spirit had not been on his side. When the other leaders decided that he had done sufficient penance, they allowed him to remove the sticks. He was then let go with respect; that is, he was held in as much esteem as before he went out to fight. If a leader came home from fighting, badly defeated, without any sorrow or crying, he was no longer held in respect but counted the very lowest man in the tribe.

If a leader had done in war all that was required of him, that is, if he had met the enemy and killed four men in the presence of both sides as witnesses, thereby winning his four feathers, he was then judged for his behavior within his Circle. He was obliged to love and respect his wife as he did himself. As was said before, he was called upon to give horses to those who needed them and he was to care for the orphans. In fact he was expected to provide for and in general defend the needy, the old, the weak, and the little ones. When the old men all were fully convinced that he was living as he should and that he had done and was doing everything in his power, without and within, for the welfare of the Circle, they made him a chief. He was never supposed to seek this high office for himself. Self-seeking was held by the Indians in great contempt.

Bands – *Wicoti*

[The basic unit of organization among the Sioux people was the *tiośpaye*, which generally included the immediate family, by blood and law, of a particular leader and those people who chose to live with him as relatives. Several tiośpayes might constitute a band of the Sioux organized for hunting or war-ring purposes. The bands were identified by nicknames with-in the larger groupings of Oglala, Yankton, Brulé, and so forth. The Oglalas and Brulés who began to live around Fort Laramie, for example, were called "loafer" bands. Saswe's band among the Yanktons was call the "Half-Breed" Band. They would gather several times a year if possible but as a rule were otherwise completely independent of the rest of the tribe.]

Whenever a move was made, the women had to attend to everything connected with the encampment. Besides tak-ing care of the tents and the provisions, cutting wood, and carrying water, there were many other things to be done. The entire charge of the "medicines" and the war equipment was left to them. The medicines were always guarded with the utmost care. Tied in bundles and wrapped in skins or cloths, they were suspended on tripods five or six feet high that were set up behind the tipis outside the Circle. It was not thought good for the medicines to have people constantly passing by them. They were held sacred and were to be kept free from impurity.

The accoutrements of war—shirts, warbonnets, shields, quivers, bows, arrows, spears, lances, guns, whips, and knives—were hung on similar tripods or poles and arranged directly in front of the tipis. They were so placed as to be within easy reach of the men, in case of a sudden attack by the enemy. In wet weather, the women covered both the medicines and the war equipment with soft buffalo robes.

Friendly bands finding themselves encamped within visiting distance of each other usually took advantage of the opportunity for contact, but even such friendly visits were accompanied with much excitement and warlike show. Horses were saddled and weapons assumed as if for actual hostilities, and the warriors made a furious advance upon the friendly encampment, riding about it, firing their guns, shooting their arrows, and imitating, as nearly as might be done with safety, the proceedings of an enemy attack. Seldom was anyone hurt in these friendly encounters, and they served not only as an opportunity for display on the part of the visitors, but also an effective warning to their hosts to be constantly on their guard lest similar incursions on the part of seemingly friendly bands might find them unprepared.

When two parties of the same or other bands were camped a little distance apart, one may not have known that the other was in the neighborhood. The party that was aware may have said: "Let us go on and sit with them," or else, "Let us go, and walk in and sit with them like Omahas." Many years ago, the Omahas had a way of entering another camp suddenly, asking for tobacco, and making themselves at home. It was from them that the Sioux got this custom.

Gathering at Rosebud, South Dakota, ca. 1889. Nebraska State
Historical Society, no. A547: 2-111.

The members of the mock-attacking party went along gaily, singing songs. As soon as they saw the camp, they sent a crier ahead to announce their approach. When he arrived, he said: "Friends, some people are coming, in fact, they are right here and they will sing and amuse you. They want to smoke your tobacco." Then the company walked in, and sat and smoked with them. If the party visited were able to do it, they gave presents of horses, clothing, and perhaps many other articles to those who came to see them.

Sometimes it happened that parties from two camps started out for a friendly raid and neither knew that the other was approaching. As the criers of each came into sight, the companies halted then and there and seated themselves on the ground. All of a sudden, they both made a mad rush forward and became intermingled. Amid the noise and confusion loud cries were heard—"I will give you this!" "We will give you that!" They continued shouting and handing around their belongings until everything on both sides was given away; as a matter of fact, one party would completely exchange goods with the other. This was called "fighting and giving away"—*ituran kicizapi*.

Another kind of "doing" among the bands was called *akicita ecipapi*, "soldiers meeting together." A band starting out to hunt buffalo would meet another bent upon the same object. Then one party would rush upon the other and fight desperately with their whips, bows, and spears. None would be killed, but many would be quite badly injured. After this [encounter], both would go together to chase the buffalo. When a mile away from the herd, they would come to a standstill and arrange themselves in two equal divisions. Eight men, called soldiers, were chosen who take positions in front of the crowd and keep them from pushing forward ahead of the others. Anyone who dared to go beyond the soldiers toward the buffalo would be severely beaten by these men or might have his horse shot under him by an arrow. If he still persisted, he was thrashed harder than ever or possibly killed on the spot. Occasionally it happened that a man succeeded in rushing past these soldiers; but he was brought back and flogged in such a manner that he was too badly injured to go to the hunt and was obliged to return to the Circle however he could. If he kept perfectly quiet and took his punishment well, he was invited by the soldiers to a dinner in camp after the hunt. They then told him that they did not want to treat him so roughly, but it was their duty to keep order and for others to obey commands. To make further amends they would perhaps give him a horse or something else of value.

*   *   *   *

When the men in the middle tent [of the Circle] had received news that a herd of buffalo was within reach, they had to decide upon the time for the hunt. In most cases it was thought better to start at once or very soon. A crier was sent through the camp, urging all the men to get ready, sharpen their arrows and their knives, have their horses saddled, and assemble. The whole band of men in feathers and war paint bearing knives, clubs, bows, and arrows then mounted their lively, knowing, little horses and rushed out of camp to the beating of drums and the singing of songs for the buffalo chase.

Two or more men acted as leaders to control the excited crowd. Sometimes a few women were allowed to go along, either because they wished to or because they were needed to help with the meat and the hides. When the band reached the place where the buffalo were grazing, the leaders called a halt. Then they looked about and chose the ground from which to start the chase.

They divided up the men, placing some on the right and the others on the left. If anyone went ahead and made a run toward the buffalo or disobeyed orders in any way, he was severely whipped and driven back. On these occasions obedience was insisted upon. No man was allowed to use a gun, as this method of killing was specifically forbidden. Any infraction of this rule was followed by a sound beating and often by the destruction of the offender's tipi. When the signal was given by the leaders, the men rushed forward upon their prey.

The buffalo saw them coming but at first made no attempt to run. They stood quietly, as if dazed, looking straight at the enemy. The noise startled them into flight. All of a sudden the whole herd turned tail and ran, with the Indians in hot pursuit. They did not stop the chase until every buffalo they needed was killed. Sometimes a buffalo, driven to fury, turned and charged, killing one or more men.

Extra horses were always brought along and left behind on the plain or in the valley until needed. At the close of the hunt, the meat and hides were loaded on them and the whole party returned to camp.

The women were kept busy slicing and sun-drying the meat. If there was not a sufficient quantity, the hunters went again to the scene of the hunt and brought back more. The night after a good hunt was most agreeable. The men sat outside their tipis and watched the meat roasting over the blazing fires and then ate their fill of the sweet, delicious food.

All that remained was stored in the hills for future use. Large holes were dug in the hillsides and in them, wrapped in the great hides, were placed the backs and other parts of the carcasses; the openings to the cavities were carefully filled up with earth. In this way the meat was well preserved and kept sweet and good for later use.

The days of the buffalo chase are past and gone. For the

Indian nothing was more exciting and exhilarating than hunting the buffalo or more enjoyable than feasting on the flesh. Tipi Sapa said to me:

> I have a terrible longing for it. You white people have come and have taken it all away from us and expect us to follow your ways. It is very hard for a people to change their whole mode of life. Now, we just sit around in camp and talk back and forth. There is nothing to do in the way of amusement, and no fun for anybody!

The old men who had no horses and were no longer able to hunt received a good share of the buffalo meat, which was given to them by the hunters. They sang the praises of these young men for their kindness and generosity, thus securing for the hunters the good opinion of everyone in camp.

SONG (OF THE OLD MEN)
A Pawnee Indian lies down
Sunrise has killed him!
Sunrise is brave!
Sunrise is brave!

ODOWAN KIN
Padani wan hed wanke do
Wihinape he econ we!
Wihinape iyahahe!
Wihinape iyahahe!

Among the Dakotas, when one of the bands was defeated in war, the members would want to take revenge but often felt they would not be successful by themselves. They therefore sent out representatives in deep mourning to go in search of help from a different band. As soon as the messengers met the friendly band they were seeking, they sat on the ground with bowed heads and covered their faces with their hands. An old man was appointed to do the speaking. He went around the group placing his hands on the head of each man in the band that was being called upon for help. As he did this, he said, "My friends, I am old. I want to take revenge on my enemies but cannot do much. Will you help us? If you do, after the battle is over, we will give you five hundred head of colts (or other valuable gifts) as a reward. Answer me! Will you help us?"

The men to whom this appeal was made pondered things for awhile; then they replied, "We will go home first, talk it over with some more of our people and let you know." They returned to their camp and related the affair to the chiefs and leaders. When they had reached a decision, they sent a message to the visitors who required assistance from them. If this decision were favorable to the latter, a great feast was held to which they were invited. Then they were told, "You lead the way because you know the country, but give us authority to attack the enemy when we see them and to fight them in our own way. If you will agree to that, we will smoke the pipe with you; if not, we will give you no help."

If the agreement was made, those who were to furnish assistance said, "Choose the time and place of meeting." The two parties met at the time and in the place appointed and started out together for the attack. When the fighting was over, the men who had been given assistance gave the promised gift to those who had helped them in the battle, and everything was arranged satisfactorily to all concerned.

Husbands and Wives

Engagements and marriages among the Indians were simple in form and lacking in ceremony. The following incident illustrates a simple form of courtship. A man had been riding a long distance on horseback and, being weary, was in a quiet, meditative mood. Lifting up his eyes he saw a comely maiden bending over a stream about to draw water, just as Isaac's servant beheld Rebekah as she was standing by the well. He alighted from his horse and stood silently gazing at the damsel. She looked at him but said nothing. They remained a long time without speaking. Then the man wandered off a little way and returned with two small sticks. One of these was thinner than the other, but both were exactly the same length. He handed the slender one to the young girl. She took it, and after breaking off a small piece, gave it back to him. This was a proposal of marriage and an acceptance. He placed the two sticks carefully together and made several specific signs which meant that at the new moon or full moon he would come to bring her to his tent and make her his wife and love her ever after.

A certain young man and young girl were in love and on the eve of being married. He talked the matter over with her and suggested that they had better wait until he had been out to fight, had killed four men, and had won his four feathers. To all this she reluctantly agreed. He had been away a long time and needed only one more feather to complete the coveted number. At last an opportunity offered. His people were expecting any moment to be attacked. With a band of men, he went to a very high cliff where they built up all the loose rocks they could find into a breastwork to protect themselves against the advancing enemy. In spite of all this, the latter rushed upon them in great numbers and overpowered them. With many others the young man was forced over the edge of the precipice and perished on the rocks below.

The young girl, when she learned that her lover was dead, put on mourning and "went about softly in the bitterness of her soul." After three or four years had elapsed, her parents urged her to marry a young man who appeared to be very desirable. She seemed to agree to it. The tipi was prepared. The young man went home in the evening, fully expecting to find his bride awaiting him. To his surprise the tent was empty. He asked several people about her and was told that she was last seen going toward the bluff. That was where the fierce fight had taken place some years before in which her former lover had met his death.

The young man, almost frantic by this time, rushed with some friends toward the spot. They saw the maiden standing on the edge of the cliff and heard her singing:

SONG
I love a young man
And I am going to be with him in spirit

ODOWAN KIN
Eca kośkanaka wan tewarinda qon
Deya wanwekdake s'a
Wanagiyata kici waun kta hunśe

As she saw the party eagerly and swiftly advancing toward her, she jumped over the precipice. Her body was mingled with the bones of the loved one she had mourned so many years. The remains of both were taken up, bound firmly and strongly together in a buffalo hide, then buried in the same spot with solemn funeral rites.

The following story can be seen as an instructive tale for young women. The story of Standing Rock was told by Paul Yellow Bear's people of North Dakota. There was a popular young girl in camp who was greatly desired as a wife by several young men, but she did not respond to the advances of any of them. One of her admirers was brave enough to propose a second time. He had met with encouragement from the girl's brother, who was strongly in favor of him. The maiden grew weary of his persistent offers and wandered off among the hills. The ardent lover pursued and found her but she paid no attention to his earnest pleadings.

When the girl's mother realized that her daughter had run away, she went immediately in search of her. She found the disdainful, cold-hearted maiden a long distance away, on a hillside. She was reclining on her right leg in what was called "the right sitting." In a faint voice, she murmured, "Mother, my body is turning into stone." The woman examined her and discovered that her legs and the lower part of her body were already petrified. In a little while, every part of the girl became perfectly rigid, as did her clothing, including her painted buffalo robe. Its colored stripes—red, white, and yellow—showed in the stone. That is the story of Standing Rock. The figure was taken to the Agency at Fort Yates and erected in a special place called "The Woman Turned into a Rock."

In choosing a wife, mere beauty was not always a consideration, since pretty girls were often believed to be of doubtful character. Young women known to be good and highly respected were the most acceptable. It was also desirable for them to be strong and healthy and able to do plenty of work.

Parents had little to do with selecting husbands for their daughters. A brother or a cousin sometimes decided who was eligible for the girls in their family. Being closely associated with the other young men in the Circle, the relatives had a fairly good knowledge of their character and social standing. One of these young men would be discussed at home. He might have met the sister of his friend before and liked her, or he might not have been personally acquainted with her. The girl would be told to dress in her finest clothes and would then be sent with a present of a number of horses to the young man's tent. This was the first and best form of matrimony and was called "marriage with horses." It was true and lasting. Nothing but death ever parted the couple united in this manner.

A young man and a girl who were acquainted and believed themselves in love could go to his tipi and live together. This second form, which was also true marriage, included couples who engaged themselves with sticks.

Sometimes a girl visited the tent of a young man she especially liked. The parents met her at the door and said, "What do you want?" She replied, "I wish to marry your son." The favored youth, who had been listening, came forward and said, "Very well, I accept you." It occasionally happened that a girl was refused. In that case, she set out to look for someone else. Such marriages of this third type were often happy and prosperous.

A fourth type was merely the case of a bad man taking a girl of ill repute to live in his tipi. She remained with him as long as she had no one else in view, but was likely to run away with the next man who noticed her and asked her to go with him. Such people were not held in any respect but were despised in the Circle.

*   *   *   *

An Indian woman was busy all the time. Her husband would say to her, "Go and do your own work. I cannot touch it. If I do I shall be pulled down and become a woman just like you." She would reply, "I do not want you to do any of my work. Just attend to your own business—hunting and fighting."

The women had to cut wood, carry water, cook the food, and take care of the children. They made the tipis, which were beautiful, as well as the handsome buckskin garments trimmed with beads and porcupine quills. It took a long time to manufacture all the accoutrements of war-shirts, warbonnets of eagles' feathers, belts, knife sheaths and cases, tobacco bags, and many other articles. The women trimmed the spears, lances, clubs, and various weapons with beads and quills. They tanned the hides of buffalo, deer, and cattle.

The tanning of buffalo hides was a long and difficult process. First the thick fat was scraped from the inside with a horn, and a mush or paste made of the brain, liver, and gall was rubbed over it again and again. The hide was turned toward the sun for a day or two and then soaked for some time in an infusion of sage brush. It was dried thoroughly and rubbed all over with a large stone. This careful preparation of the hide made it soft and pliable.

The women had entire charge of everything connected with moving camp from one place to another. They were obliged to care for the tents, the medicines, and the war outfits; to saddle the horses for the men; and to carry the meat

Preparing rawhide. Nebraska State Historical Society,
no. A547: 2-226.

and other provisions. No wonder it is so impressed upon our minds that the Indian woman did all the work!

The parents of the first or true wife sometimes thought she ought to have more help. They suggested that a sister should go to live with her in order to share the burden of the work. In this way, the latter became a wife as well. Even with two wives, the amorous spirit of the Indian was not always contented. In roving about, he would meet some girl he fancied, talk with her a little while, and finally ask her to go to his tipi to live with him and his family. This arrangement generally seemed acceptable to her. Second and third wives were looked upon merely as helpers.

A man and woman married according to the first type were as a rule true to one another until death parted them. An exception happened, however, in the case of Chief Charger, who lived on Standing Rock Reservation. A man ran off with his wife and was living in constant dread of the chief. It was the opinion of the young men of the tribe that at such a time the husband should seek out the offender and fight him; in that way he would prove himself to be a true brave. The advice of the old men was just the opposite. They thought that a higher courage would be shown by the husband, were he to go to the man who had wronged him, and talk to him quietly, somewhat as follows: "You need not be afraid of me. Keep my wife—perhaps she loves you, and you love her." Chief Charger followed the latter course and not only surrendered his wife at her desire but also gave to the man who had wronged him a number of horses and other gifts, among them—and more difficult to part with—his warbonnet and his coat of finest buckskin trimmed with hairs.

The following story is told of a woman married according to the second form. She had for a long time been badly treated by a brutal husband. Unable to endure it any longer, she ran away from home. She wandered about, up hill and down dale, for many months until her moccasins were worn to rags and her feet were badly swollen. She finally became so exhausted from suffering, but chiefly from want of food, that she lay down on a hillside expecting to die.

After a little while she noticed that something was sniffing about her, but she felt too weak to turn her head to see what it was or to offer any resistance if she were in danger. Presently, without lifting her head, she perceived that a wolf was slinking off into the distance. A few minutes later, she saw this same wolf coming back with three others. They crept up softly and stealthily and examined her closely. Finding that the woman's blanket was wrapped about her very loosely, they dragged it off and spread it flat on the ground. They placed her upon it, "by bite," and each one of them took a corner of the blanket in his mouth. Then the wolves trotted away bravely with their burden to a rocky cave in the timberland.

In those days people were near to the animals and on friendly terms with them. This woman seemed to understand the nature of the wolves and to know that they were not to be feared except when they were driven mad in times of famine or prolonged snow. Her captors treated her with great kindness. Whenever a fine sheep or calf was brought home, it was torn open at once and the liver and kidneys were taken out and given to her to nibble upon. After a while, the woman regained her strength.

She made friends with the families of the wolves living in these rocky caverns, and she used to enjoy playing with the fluffy little cubs as much as they did with her. She got to know the language of the wolves and liked to see them smile and laugh. She remained with them a long time and began to feel quite at home. One day, she received a formal visit from several of them. They said to her, "Your people are about. They will find out our dens and attack and kill us for our skins. We are going away and shall leave you behind." She made motions to them, trying to ask them what she could do in return for all their kindness. They understood and replied, "See that we get some fat to eat." Then they left her and went their way.

The woman wandered back to her own people and sought out her mother's tipi. She told the story of her troubles and of all the kindness she had received from the wolves. She also expressed a strong desire to give them what they had asked for. A crier was told to proclaim it in camp. After the next buffalo chase, a great pile of fat was collected and handed over to her. The woman had it carried a long distance away to some hills. Then she howled like a wolf. The wolves recognized her voice and knew what it meant to them. They all came forward, had a delicious meal, and carried the remainder of the fat to their homes. The woman continued to give them food at intervals for many years; and she and the wolves were fast friends. She was called Living in the Rocks Woman, and she died about thirty years ago [around 1885].

The following story is an illustration of the punishment inflicted upon a pair of lovers who dishonored the second form of marriage. A certain young couple had been living together about four months and were apparently happy. The husband was called away for a little while and upon his return in the evening, he was surprised not to find his wife in the tipi. He soon learned that she had run away with another man. He pondered over the matter, but resolved not to do anything until the next morning.

Then, rising early, he painted his face with various colors, armed himself with a gun and bow and arrows, mounted his horse, and rode off in search of the guilty pair. The injured man had not gone far before he discovered their tracks. He followed them and soon caught up with his wife and her lover. Upon seeing him, the latter asked what he wanted. The husband replied, "I have come after my wife. We will fight. If I kill you I will take her back; if you kill me, you can have her for your own."

They fought first at some distance apart with guns, then with bows and arrows, taking aim, drawing, and coming nearer and nearer to one another. The guilty man was sorely wounded, being pierced through the lungs with an arrow, and blood gushed from his mouth. His honor satisfied, the woman's husband took his wife home, cut off her hair close to her head, and ordered her to walk away from him with her clothes partly removed. When she had gone a certain distance, he shot at her, wounding her in the upper part of the leg. After this disgraceful conduct and its ensuing punishment, the woman never went again inside the Circle. None of the other women would associate with her, and she was obliged to wander about "all her years in the bitterness of her soul." She died seven or eight years ago [around 1908].

After a time, her lover was brought home. For several months, he suffered terribly from his wound for several months and finally died in agony. A piece of buffalo fat was placed in the mouth of such a man, and he was buried face downward. His spirit was bad and was not allowed to disturb the tribe as it had while he was in the world. This would be impossible if he were facing downward toward the center of the earth. Because the husband of the wretched woman had committed murder, he was obliged to paint himself mud color and for a long time afterward was not allowed to go into the Circle.

If the men happened to be smoking the pipe and he suddenly made his appearance, they did not hand it to him; but

Woman with hitching team at a temporary camp, ca. 1892. Nebraska State Historical Society, no. A547: 2-152.

if by any chance he got hold of it to smoke, he had the humiliation of seeing the next man who handled it wipe off the stem of the pipe. It would have been far better for the unfortunate individual who lost his wife in such a way to follow the advice of the old men: "Let her go; leave her alone. If you follow her, and try to be avenged, you make yourself wicked, too."

There was a more simple and perhaps less painful method of ridding oneself of a wife or a husband, and it constituted absolute divorce among the Dakota Nation. When a great crowd assembled in the Circle for a dance, a man would step forward. He would point to a woman standing beside him and shout, "There is the woman who has been my wife! After this, she can carry water for any of you. She is free!" This man was obliged to keep his word and was never to try to get his wife back again. If he did, he was looked upon with great contempt. A husband was freed in a similar manner. The wife, assisted by another woman, sang the following song: The "friend" to whom she referred was, of course, her husband.

SONG

My friend, go away!
I shall follow thee no more!

ODOWAN KIN

Koda, iyaya yo!
Wau kte śni ye do!

It was the sad fate of many a woman to lose her husband in war. The afflicted widow proceeded at once to lower her dress in the neck and to shorten it at the bottom. She then cut off her hair and made gashes in her neck and legs. These signs of deep mourning signified that she intended to be true to her husband and never to marry a second time. In order to make this known, she walked repeatedly around the Circle and stirred up the sympathy of the people by her forlorn appearance.

Tipi Sapa knew of a woman whose husband was killed in battle. She was about twenty years old at the time and was left with a little daughter. He said that whenever her hair grew out, she sheared it off, and she gashed her neck and legs over and over again. There came a time, however, when she ceased to do these things. She allowed her hair to grow to quite a length, and parted and arranged it very neatly. Then she put on her best shawl and went to talk with some of her friends.

Upon seeing her improved appearance, they looked at her in surprise. She said to them, "You suppose I am thinking of some man, but I am not. Things are now to be just as I want them. I dreamed last night that my husband was talking to me and he said, 'You and the daughter will soon be with me.' That means I shall die soon." She then went to her log house. A night or two afterward, a cousin came to visit. The widow gave her a bed in the corner and made up one for her little daughter and herself directly in the center of the room. During the night, the heavy ridgepole that supported the log house fell and brought down the roof with it. Both mother and daughter were instantly killed. The dream had come true. The sorrowful widow and the little daughter were once more united with the husband and father.

A woman's father-in-law and mother-in-law were obliged to be most careful not to say anything that would offend or hurt the feelings of their daughter-in-law. Great evil and sorrow might be the result. A son-in-law was supposed never to see or to look toward his mother-in-law. If he did, he was considered a bad man. Neither must a woman ever look at her son-in-law. They could have seen one another before they became connected by marriage, but they

A woman working with porcupine quills, ca. 1893. Nebraska State Historical Society, no. A547: 2-155.

were never to let it happen again. It was also most important that a brother should respect his sister. A girl in a family should rather die than have unkind reflections cast upon her by a brother; in the same way a son-in-law was obliged to respect his mother-in-law.

The following story is an illustration of the regard shown by a son-in-law for his mother-in-law. It deals with an Indian named Bone Club, who once lived in the neighborhood of Wakpala on Standing Rock Reservation, South Dakota. He had his tipi at one time very near that of his wife's parents, but the opening faced in the opposite direction. A little way beyond and almost between the tipis was a corral cut from cottonwood trees. Inside were the horses of both families. A warrior who was considered a prophet predicted that a horse would soon be taken from this corral by a Crow Indian. The same man would be seen falling from the horse "with bloods" (that is, with drops of blood).

That very night, a noise was heard outside the tipis. The father-in-law, thinking he heard his son, Black Bear, returning home, called out, "Is that you, my son?" Immediately there was a shot, and with a groan the old man fell dead. Bone Club felt that it was his duty to die rather than let his mother-in-law be harmed. On hearing the shot he rushed from the tipi in time to see a Crow Indian ride away on one of the horses. Bone Club ran after him and shot at him several times. The next morning, as prophesied, the horse was seen with a man falling from him, and blood drops stained the snow. It was the Crow Indian who had ridden between the tipis, shot down the old man, and stolen the horse.

The following story also illustrates the respect of sons-in-law for mothers-in-law. A man named Big Head, hearing a noise in the night, rushed from his tipi and found that his mother-in-law's horse had been stolen. He saw a man riding away at full speed. He mounted his own horse and followed the man very closely. Big Head drew his bow again and again until he had stuck the object of pursuit full of arrows. The man was overcome and fell down from the stolen horse. The night was intensely dark with not even a star to be seen. Big Head took flint and steel; with the soft wood which he carried in his leather belt he made a light. He found that his victim, though bristling with arrows, was still alive. Big Head seized him by the hair and with a great sharp knife cut off his head at the throat. Carrying the grim trophy home in triumph, he placed it on a pole outside of his tipi.

Sons and Daughters

Indian children were expected to remember everything their parents said to them. It was especially impressed upon their minds never to tell a lie, and they were counseled as follows: "You may live to be old, you may reach middle age, you may die young, we do not know. That is in the hands of the Giver; but in any case, be truthful as long as you live. Then you must be pure and modest and honorable so that people will respect you."

All Indian children were tattooed, the girls on the chin or forehead, the boys sometimes on the torso, but more frequently on the wrist or some other part of the arm. This custom was carefully observed because of an old tradition. In the days of the wisest men, the "Milky Way" was thought to be the high road of the Spirits, which led them either toward the happy hunting grounds to the right, or to the left and the abode of punishment. An old man sat along the way to watch the spirits of the dead as they approached. When he saw the spirits of tattooed children draw near, he directed them to the right; but turned the poor little wanderers without tattoos toward the left-hand road.

GIRLS

In those days, girls seem to have paid attention to all the precepts taught them by their parents and to have obeyed them without a murmur. Very often the poorer class of girls followed the instruction of the old people better than those of more prosperous families. The daughters liked to be with their mothers and always remained with them until they were married. As a rule the Indian girls became good wives—pure, true, and upright. They were kept very busy, as they made the tipis, their own dresses, and the fighting and hunting outfits for the men in the family. They trimmed all this clothing with beautiful beadwork and porcupine quills.

Both the girls who paid attention to the good teachings and those who did not had the gift of healing and were equally successful. There were many medicine women who sucked the disease from the skin of anyone who was ill. They also had the gift of conjury and were eagerly sought after as fortune-tellers. Tipi Sapa could not understand why the bad as well as the good should be endowed with these gifts and meet with success. He thought the former should have been punished with failure at every turn.

The Circle was not free from gossip. Often a girl was made very unhappy by hearing something that had been said against her character. At such a time she brought a dish of food from her tipi and took a seat in the Circle. She invited all the other girls of good standing to bring their dishes and join her in camp. They dared not go if they were of doubtful reputation. A large crowd assembled to witness the test called Innocent's Fire. An arrow and a knife were plunged into the ground and a small painted rock was placed near them. A rock was sacred among the Indians and one of the means by which prayers reached the Great Spirit.

A certain young man was called upon to step forward. He had perhaps remarked, "Well, this girl promised to marry me but she lied," or something to that effect. Then he was obliged to take the arrow and the knife out of the ground and draw them across his lips and place his hands on the rock. If he himself had been telling an untruth in speaking ill of the girl in question, he was likely to meet his death very shortly afterward in one of three ways. He might be killed by an arrow, stabbed with a knife, or injured fatally in stumbling over a rock. This seldom failed to happen. By going into the Circle in such a manner the girl proved her innocence.

Sometimes a young woman of fine character called a meeting at her tipi of all the girls of good reputation from prosperous families in camp and gave them a feast. There was much talking back and forth on these occasions. "How many times have you been through 'Innocent's Fire'?" one asked. Perhaps somebody answered, "Twice"; another, "Three times," another "Five times," and so on. They spoke beautifully of their mothers, and said that any virtue in themselves was owing to the good teaching they had received from them. These girls generally remained a long while at the meeting, exhorting one another "to love and to do good works." They laid great stress upon being kind to the poor and also agreed to look after their weaker sisters in the Circle to try to keep them from going astray. These meetings were bound to have good results because their influence was direct and far-reaching.

It was especially harmful for a brother, cousin, father-in-law, or mother-in-law to think any evil of a girl belonging to the family; it did not matter so much about the opinion of the other relatives and connections. By way of illustration, an incident such as the following has happened many times. A certain young man heard by chance an unpleasant story

Nebraska State Historical Society, no. A547: 2-228.

about his sister. When he went home, he found the poor innocent girl, contented and happy, singing over the bead-work with which she was busily engaged. "You are bad! I am ashamed of you!" he declared bluntly.

The girl, not being able to endure such remarks, ran off without saying a word. She was absent so long that her mother became alarmed and started out to look for her. The poor woman had not gone far before she met someone running in great haste toward the camp. It proved to be a friend of her daughter's who had just come through the timber. She reported that she had just seen the unfortunate girl, with a lasso around her neck, hanging from the branch of a tree. Tipi Sapa had several sisters and other women relatives. His constant care was to avoid making thoughtless, unkind remarks about them for fear of the consequences.

When a girl reached the age of sixteen, she was put in a tipi by herself and remained there four days. Her mother carried food and water to her. The woman acknowledged as the best in the tribe gave her advice and talked to her of the things that would bring her honor.

BOYS

While a boy was yet a tiny baby he was taken by his father to a man to have his ears pierced. Fairly good-sized slits were cut with a sharp knife in the lobe of the ear and pieces of lead inserted to prevent the holes from growing together until the boy was old enough to wear earrings. A girl had her ears pierced at the top as well as in the lower part and wore large earrings in each of the openings.

Indian boys were carefully instructed by their fathers in regard to the Great Spirit and all the lesser spirits who were his helpers. It was their first duty to try to gain the friendship of one of these minor spirits. They were trained to harden themselves to all kinds of harsh conditions, including bitter cold and terrible fatigue. They were compelled to walk with the men for miles through heavy snowdrifts in the face of a biting wind. Sometimes they would be caught in a raging blizzard such as Tipi Sapa himself encountered.

When he was a little boy, he went with a number of men a long distance from camp to help bring back some buffalo that had been killed. The party battled with the icy wind and blinding snow and floundered about in the huge drifts for two days and two nights. Suddenly Tipi Sapa discovered that he had lost his moccasins! This made no difference to him, however. He continued on his way for a distance of four miles with bare feet. They were not frost bitten—it seemed almost a miracle. The rapid circulation caused by the constant and violent exercise must have prevented injury.

The following was another method for cultivating endurance and was, besides, a practice in praying. A young man started out with a friend to look for the skull of a buffalo. One carried a pipe and the other, a lasso. When they found the skull, they fastened the lasso firmly around it and one of them placed it several yards away. Then the young man lay on the ground while his companion pulled up the skin from his back across the shoulders, cut four holes in it with a knife, ran the lasso through them and tied it. The youth was now ready to start. Carrying the pipe, he dragged the buffalo's head all the way back to camp. Sometimes it got caught in rough places, on stones, twigs, and branches and had to be jerked loose. The young man turned around every little while, with the pipe in his hand, and prayed to the skull. The rope fastened into his shoulders would usually break through the flesh. If not, he was obliged to drag the skull back to the distant place in which he found it. The young man often had visions during this procedure. It was supposed to make him successful in buffalo hunting.

There was a special way of [training boys] in connection with "the spirit of the buffalo." A boy belonging to one of the best families in camp was called to the middle tent, or place of honor, in which the leading people lived. The principal man then asked him to go out and hunt buffalo. Perhaps five or six others were sent with him, and he was appointed their leader. They went through all the surrounding country. As they returned toward camp, and were as close as five miles away, they flashed a mirror. If they had no mirror and happened to be on a high butte or hill, they made one of the party ride up and down so as to be plainly seen. All this meant that they were bringing good news. Then the people in the middle tent began to sing gaily the song of the wolves (Wolf Society):

SONG
Friend, behold me!
I am the man who looks
As the wolves look at things!

ODOWAN KIN
Koda, wanmayake ye!
Šunka wakita qon
Miye yedo!

It sometimes happened that two or three of those who went out with the boy leader determined to go on ahead and tell the people they had seen buffalo. When they reached camp, they were not received by the older men. The honored boy had to appear first and tell them the exact truth.

When the party arrived, either on horseback or on foot, they went at once to the middle tent. There sat the leader with possibly as many as twelve other men in conclave, for all the good men had to be present. The questioner or leading man was always to the right of the boy. He said to him, "You know all the country. Where did you go? What did you see beyond?" He took the pipe and pointed it to heaven, to the four corners of the winds, and to the earth. He handed it to the youth. The latter touched it with his lips but did not smoke it. This act was equivalent to an oath to speak the truth.

The boy gave it back to the leading man, who smoked it and passed it along to the others. The time had come for the boy leader to make an absolutely truthful statement about what he had seen of the buffalo. He was about to point with his forefinger to indicate the place, but was told to use his thumb instead. The boy then had to point with his thumb in three directions, in front, to the right, and to the left, and was obliged to tell what he had seen in the places indicated. Then he was asked if he had seen some other things, but could do what he pleased about relating anything more. He was compelled to answer the first three questions only. He had brought back with him "the spirit of the buffalo," and all the men present had to receive it to ensure that they would be successful in the next chase.

HONORING CHILDREN

It was the custom for a father to declare that he wanted his children "honored" on a certain day. After he had chosen a man to perform the ceremony, he said to him, "Will you honor my daughter? If you do, I will give you fifteen head of horses." The man, after thinking the matter over, might finally agree to it. This decision reached, he went about his duties at once.

First he tried to find some fine clothes for the girl who was to be honored. If possible, he procured a buckskin suit trimmed with beads, as well as several rows of elks' teeth, which were considered both beautiful and valuable. From under the wing of an eagle, he took a soft feather and tied it with a strip of antelope skin, making an ornament for the girl's hair. A girl could be honored more than once; and she sometimes received as many as four eagles' feathers.

After securing these things, the man who was appointed to do the honoring erected a special tent for the ceremony and chose seven men to take part. Two of them were to carry a rattle and an imitation pipe in either hand. (An Indian rattle was made by wrapping a piece of rawhide around a ball of clay that served as a mold. When dry the clay was removed and pebbles were placed inside the rawhide form.) Five other men were also selected, besides drummers and singers.

They all met together and went toward the lodge of the man whose daughter or daughters were to be honored. They shook the rattles, beat, the drums, and sang the following:

SONG
Where are they living?

ODOWAN KIN
Tukted tipi he?

All this was intended to show that the girls were good and worthy of being held in honor. The men who were appointed to carry the clothing went with the honoring man into the tipi. They were likely to find a warbonnet and a shirt made of weasels' skins hanging over the entrance. In those days a weasel-skin shirt was very valuable, being worth fully five hundred dollars. The men could not touch these articles if they had never before given away things of this kind on such an occasion.

There might be a man among the others outside who had given away such things at a time of honoring; he would have a right to go in and get them. If the man whose children were being honored was later part of a ceremony for the children of someone else, he was allowed to take valuable things of this sort himself, having given such things away.

The door of the tipi was opened, and the five men who had been selected went in. The weasel-skin shirt and the warbonnet were taken. Several of the five men placed the girls on their backs and all went out toward the large tent in the middle of the Circle. Around this a great crowd was assembled. The girls were carried inside the tent and the entrance was closed. A man came forward and painted red lines down their foreheads, signifying that they should try to be good. They were dressed in their fine clothing, and the eagles' feathers were placed in their hair. The tent was then opened so that everyone could see them. The two men carrying the imitation pipes and the rattles waved the pipes over their heads, shook the rattles, and sang:

SONG
The West Wind knows
These people are blessed
The North wind knows
These people are blessed
The South Wind knows
These people are blessed
The East Wind knows
These people are blessed
The Earth knows
These people are blessed

The Creator knows
These people are blessed

ANOTHER FORM OF THE ABOVE
Bless the West
Bless the North
Bless the East
Bless the South
Bless the Earth
Bless the Creator

ODOWAN KIN
Wiyorpeyata kin sdodya
Dena wicayawaśtepi kin
Waziyata kin sdodya
Dena wicayawaśtepi kin
Itokaga kin sdodya
Dena wicayawaśtepi kin
Hinyanpata kin sdodya
Dena wicayawaśtepi kin
Makata kin sdodya
Dena wicayawaśtepi kin
Wankata kin sdodya
Dena wicayawaśtepi kin

WANKATA KIN ED OECON
TOKECA WAN YUKAN
Wiyorpeyata kin waśte
Waziyata kin waśte
Hinyanpata kin waśte
Itokaga kin waśte
Makata kin waśte
Wankata kin waśte

After the songs, the girls turned around toward the open door. The singers pounded their drums quickly while the two men danced furiously, keeping time to the music. This was the finishing touch to the ceremony.

A great deal was expected of the young people who had been honored and blessed. They were supposed henceforth to live up to all that they had been taught; to do all the good that was in their power; and to be true, just, pure, and honorable. They had as well the right to put on their fine clothes whenever they wished and to decorate themselves with the same paint marks. All these things proved that they had been honored; but it was considered far better for them to show the honoring by the lives they led. Anyone who attempted to dress and paint in this way without having gone through the ceremony of being honored was held in great contempt.

Boys were honored in the same manner except that on such occasions four men were chosen to represent the four winds. The man who talked to the boys said in addition to what had been told the girls: "Now you must honor the Earth, as it is the footstool of the Great Spirit and His floor that you walk upon. The Great Spirit will guide you. Live as you have been directed before these witnesses—the Great Spirit, His footstool, and the four Winds." The men who had done the honorings received horses or other valuables in consideration of their services.

There was still another way of honoring a daughter. The father made a number of balls and painted them red. When there was no fighting, red was a sign of peace. The daughter threw ten or fifteen balls from the door of her tipi into a crowd assembled in the circle. Whoever caught a ball would receive a horse. If one man was fortunate enough to catch two or three of the balls, he received as many horses.

Sometimes a man wished to honor a daughter who had died in order to keep her spirit near him as long as possible. Such honoring took place only in the best families. Selecting something that had belonged to her—perhaps her work-bag containing needles, beads, and porcupine quills, he tied it up in a very fine skin and placed it on a tripod in one corner of the closed tipi. Part of any food that was cooked was put aside for her. When he had done this for three or four months, he took a stake and drove it into the ground. At the top of the stake he fastened a picture, as nearly as he could reproduce it, of the daughter's face. Then, having placed all her good clothes and other belongings near the stake, he opened the tipi and invited his friends and neighbors in to a feast.

Meantime he had selected a friend to represent him on this occasion. He sat there quietly while a third man acted as master of ceremonies. The latter told the people who had assembled that now the soul of the daughter was leaving the tipi and going to the spirit world. He said that all present must ever remember this day. They must try to be pure, true, merciful, and humble, and to lead upright lives as long as they were in this world. They had witnessed all that had been done by this family to make people good, and it was their duty to teach these things to their children.

The friend who represented the father was awarded a prize, which was likely to be the finest horse. The master of ceremonies received a handsome gift, as did all the others in turn. The father of the girl whose memory had been held in honor was bound after this ceremonial to be a helpful man in his tribe. It made him of much more importance in the circle and gave him wider influence.

The young women as well as the men sought his advice. If anything went wrong, it was his duty to set it right. A certain party in the tribe might be preparing to fight with some others who did not wish to be drawn into the contest. The people would say, "Why do you not call in this wise man to make the decision?" It was the duty of the latter to persuade the disputants to forget their differences and to try to live in peace.

Games

The Indians were fond of all kinds of sport and enjoyed games of a mild character as well as those that were more thrilling and dangerous. The game of shinny was among the most popular, and both men and women entered into the contest. As many as two hundred at a time lined up for this sport, the large number adding greatly to the mirth, excitement, and general interest. [Shinny was a Plains version of the eastern lacrosse or the Choctaw ball game and was played with the same enthusiasm. It involved a hard leather ball and sticks comparable to hockey sticks with which the players struck the ball. Goals were set and scores were made when one team pushed or hit the ball across a goal.]

The game called "strike the moccasins" or *hanpapa econpi* was for men alone. We will suppose that two parties were camping two or three miles apart and one sent word to the other, saying, "Let us go over and strike the moccasins." If everything seemed favorable, a large tipi was prepared. The men from both camps took their guns, horses, and arrows and marched over to this tipi, beating drums and singing as they went along:

SONG
Whatever widows make
[belongs] to me!

ODOWAN KIN
Wiwazica taku kage cin
Hena mitawa ye!

They also sang many songs without words, waved their arms, and made wild gestures. They went into the tipi and each party took one side of it. A large crowd stood outside and lifted up the sides in order to see the game. In winter, fires were blazing around the tipi to keep the people warm.

When the parties were ready to play, each side chose one man. Each side also picked out one little ball about the size of a marble, and of the same color—red, black, or yellow. Then a man was selected to start the game. When the signal was given him by the umpire, he took both of the balls in his hands, stood up, and said, "I choose so and so (naming a man) in my place. I am so brave... (he went on to tell what he had done in former games). Have the courage to be laughed at. Take this ball and hide it so that the others cannot find it." The man chosen from the other party received the other ball and was given the same instructions.

The men chosen in both parties took the balls in their hands and sang, gesticulated, and threw them about as a sleight-of-hand performer does. Another man, standing some seven to ten feet away, watched them and tried to guess where the ball was. He was called "the striker of the moccasins." The players watched him too, very intently, as he made various motions. Sometimes he closed down three fingers, leaving the thumb and forefinger open. That signified that he thought the balls were in the outside hands of each player. When he put his hand straight down with the thumb up, he thought the balls were in the right hand of one man and in the left of the other. If he motioned with two fingers, he meant that the balls were in the left hands of each. When he made a sign with one finger, he indicated that the balls were in the right hand of each man. If the striker of the moccasins guessed correctly, the players had to show him the balls. When he found out both of them in one guess, he could take the balls from the men and give them to whomsoever he wished on his side to continue the game.

At the beginning of the game, each party had twelve sticks. If the man chosen to do the guessing happened to miss, his side lost a stick. One of the parties may have acquired a great many sticks; but if a player on the winning side let the ball drop from his hand to the ground, the other side could claim all the sticks won. The party that took all the sticks won the game. Various goods were wagered—warbonnets, shirts, bows, arrows, quivers, and other articles. These were divided among the members of the winning team.

All of the Sioux Nation played the game in this manner, except the Santee band, who used moccasins. As soon as the game was called, it proceeded with the same sleight of hand, but those who had the balls took off their moccasins and covered them with a corner of their blankets. This prevented the people from seeing whether both balls were put into one moccasin or one into each moccasin. The man who watched the play then took a stick and struck the moccasins in which he thought the balls were placed.

Among games for women was one called "throwing sticks"—*paslo hanpi unpi*. Each player had a stick seven feet long with a buffalo or an elk horn fastened to one end. In order to make it fit tightly, the horn was boiled and placed on the stick while it was still soft. In the winter when the snow was hard and slippery, a number of young girls went out in the open with these sticks and lined up with perhaps four, five, or six on a side. They took turns throwing or sliding their sticks as far as they could over the frozen snow. The side having the larger number of those who threw them the longer distance won the game and all the beadwork of their opponents as well.

Another winter game for women was *icaśdahe kicunpi*, "using the balls." Several girls, perhaps as many as eight, went off together to a creek or river that was frozen over. They took some small cylindrical pieces of wood about two inches in height and the same in diameter and a few little wooden balls. After they had built fires, they spread their robes on the ice and sat down for the game about twenty feet from the opposing side. One of the small, round pieces of wood was put before each player. All in turn tried to hit these with the little balls, each one aiming at the piece in front of the girl directly across from her. If she succeeded in hitting it, she could compel the girl opposite to give up a piece of her bead or porcupine quill work.

The game went on until all the goods played for were handed over to the winning side. The girls liked to play this game, and did so whenever they had an opportunity. Although it was played some distance from the camp or village, the young men usually found out the place where the girls intended to go and were sure to be on hand to view the game. In this way there was much merriment, not to mention courting, and lively entertainment for all concerned.

[The following activity seemed to the writer to be merely a game, but it was actually a method of attracting the spirit of particular animals.]

A great circle about a mile in diameter in which thousands could assemble was prepared, and in it was placed a huge tent. In the circle too was a roaring fire over which a great pot was boiling. In this was thrown a buffalo's tongue or a deer's tongue, or a fish. Large quantities of other things also were boiling and steaming in the pot. It was carefully watched by a man who knew secret things. Many of the people rubbed themselves all over with a kind of root that kept them from being scalded by the boiling contents of the pot. Then, with a mad rush, they all began to dance around the kettle and sing songs.

SONG
Little Wind belongs to me!
In this kettle they place
A deer tongue for me!

ODOWAN KIN
Tate Ciqayena mitawa nunwe!
Cega de ed taceji wan iyorpeyapi e
Mitawa nunwe!

After this a man called out, "It is not time yet," which actually was a signal that everything was ready. Immediately all pressed violently forward and tried to grab something from the steaming pot, while they shouted and yelled, "Don't come over here with that boiling stuff!"—meaning quite the opposite. Whereupon they ran madly about, throwing the hot soup all over one another.

The men who got the buffalo tongue or the deer tongue or the fish were the ones who would know secret things that would help them in hunting or catching these animals. As may be imagined, those who joined in this sport were covered from head to foot with the hot grease. A clean white skin hanging up a little distance away afforded an opportunity for the crowd to rid themselves of some of the mess, until the skin was in the same condition as themselves. Whereupon the players took a swim in the nearby creek and in that way cleaned and cooled themselves before returning to camp.

Societies

In the Circle were many societies, and men who did not belong to one of these groups had no standing whatever. The societies were somewhat alike in their offices and duties. The Society of Braves, *Cante Tinza Okodakiciye*, held a large meeting every year in the middle tent. Seven principal men represented this society and there were, besides, a doorkeeper and a crier who proclaimed a dance, feast, or any other doings.

The seven chief officers gave their decision as to new members and sent men through the camp to get them. If the young men were found in their tipis, they were taken by the arm and brought out. Four or six girls of fine character were selected to help with the singing. All went in procession with singing to the place of meeting, where they were received by the seven principal men.

The new members were presented with various articles. Two were given warbonnets with feathers reaching the ground. Two others received whips; two others, clubs; and one, a drum. Then the officers talked to them, relating what each of them had done with these same things. Each new member was compelled to live up to the high standard of the society. He had to be pure and true, as well as generous, giving horses to the poor, to orphans, and to old people. If it were found out that a new member had done wrong—for instance, going off with the wife of another man, he was dropped from the society. Above all else, each one was required to be brave, go out to fight, and be willing to lose his life.

SONG
One of the members
Does not return home

ODOWAN KIN
Opapi kin etanhan
Wanji kdi śni

The Society of Owls' Feathers, *Mawatani Okodakiciye*, like that of the Braves, had seven chief officers, a doorkeeper, and a crier. It was composed of older and more experienced men of a very high order. The members wore plumes of owls' feathers in their hair. They made these plumes by taking the long feathers from the wing or tail of the owl, pulling off the downy feathers from the middle, and tying them in bunches on sticks.

Two of the seven principal men had warbonnets made of owls' feathers, two others had spears, two had whips, and one a drum. The seven principal men held office twelve months at a time, and if they had done well were re-elected. New members were chosen after the same manner as in the Society of Braves, and also a few young women were selected to help with the singing. The following song was sung by two men as the new members were marched to the middle tent:

SONG
I hear there are hard things
To be accomplished.
I seek them.

ODOWAN KIN
Wicoran qeya terike do
Eyapi e
Hena awakita yedo.

When the time had come for the election of officers, the name of a new member was called. He was told to stand at some distance until asked to go forward by one of the leading men. Then another man placed a coal of fire in his hand. With this he was obliged to walk slowly and steadily toward the officer who was to present him with a warbon-net, spear, and whip. Each new member was called in turn. When the new members had received their respective belongings, they were addressed by the leading men. It was expected of them to maintain the high moral standard of the society. They were never to scold or whip their wives, as anything of that kind was an indication of weakness. If they lowered themselves to fight with women they were just like them.

Should the wife of one of these men run away with someone else, her husband was not allowed to go after her to bring her back. She was to be left alone, as her character was gone and she could never again take her place in the Circle. When it happened that a wife of a member of this society did run off with another man, but came back of her own accord, her husband had to receive her and treat her kindly as before. This was the song that was sung by a man when his wife left him.

SONG

My daughter's (or son's) mother
Goes away from me
I have but a short time to live!

ODOWAN KIN

Micunkśi (naiś micinkśi)
Hunkuya ko eyaya yo
Nankenunna waun we!

SECOND SONG

You will never be buried
With your wife's body
Only dogs fight over a female
You are a man

ODOWAN INONPA KIN

Tukted nunke cinhan
Kici nunkin kte śni
Śunka ecena win okicize cin
Winica yedo

This song was a curse upon the woman who ran away. The man was to behave better than a dog and not fight with the wretch who went with her. Only dogs got mad and fought. The afflicted husband was marched in procession around the circle while the songs were sung. All this was intended to lighten his burden and relieve his distress.

The members of the Society of Owls' Feathers were supposed to give liberally to the poor, the aged, and orphans. They were schooled to endure severe hardships. They had to go out and fight and do everything else in

their power outside the circle for the welfare and advance-
ment of the tribe. The newly elected member sang:

SONG
See me! I am trying
To follow the teachings of the
Society of Owls' Feathers
Because I do not want
To reach old age

ODOWAN KIN
Mawatani Okodakiciye kin
Hecel eyapi e,
Econ uwata nunwe.
Icin wicarcapi kin he
Tamonka śni yedo

A big dinner or feast was held at the annual meeting,
followed by a dance, so as to give the people the opportunity of getting acquainted with the new members.

Another group was called the Society of Foxes. The
members wore their hair in a very distinctive manner. Most
of the hair was pulled out by the roots, leaving the scalp bare
except for patches or tufts in front, on either side, and in the
middle. The middle section was allowed to grow very long so
that it could be braided to hang down the back. Ornaments
consisting of two sticks about a foot in length, with bright
red feathers glued on them, were worn in the hair at the top
of the braid. The long locks of hair on either side of the head
were drawn through a cylinder of bone. Where the hair came
through, the bone cylinders were decorated with weasels'
skins. The faces of foxes were also used for ornaments. The
skin was pulled off the face so that the bones and teeth

showed plainly. The faces were painted red or blue and were fastened in rows on buckskin or some kind of leather bands and worn around the forehead in the dance.

The Society of Foxes conducted itself in much the same way as those of the Braves and Owls' Feathers. At the yearly meeting the officers sat in the place prepared for them in the middle of the Circle. The new members, with a few women, were gathered together and marched into their presence while this song was sung:

SONG
My friend has passed his life
Doing his duty before me
So I will follow him!

ODOWAN KIN
Mitakoda taku econ
Kta iyececa kin econ
Un mitokam iyaya e
Ehakenan waun we!

When they were seated, the new members were called forward by the principal men and presented with the marks of office. Two received bows with no strings but trimmed with beadwork and porcupine quills. On one end of the bows were fastened spearheads, which were used as weapons. Two others had pipes of peace given them, two more received whips, and another a drum. If the former office holders were re-elected, they received the same articles again. The doorkeeper and crier had no marks of office. After this, the new men were instructed in their duties. They were obliged to be liberal and very brave. They had to do everything possible outside for the welfare of the circle. If they failed in their duties, within or without, they were dropped from the society.

The members of the Grass Society were all warriors. They placed dried grass in their moccasins to keep their feet warm and carried it in their clothing to be used when they wanted to build a fire quickly. They wore their hair cut off on either side, leaving it long in the middle for the braid. A second braid was fastened in at the end, so as to make it of great length. At the top of the braid were fastened various small objects, such as the tail of a deer, dyed red, and eagles' feathers corresponding to the number of men killed by the warrior. Sometimes the feathers were so numerous that they were stuck in the braid as well and often extended through the whole length of it to the ground.

In some cases a spear with its head painted red was carried, and on the end of it were tied three or more feathers according to the number of enemies the owner had killed. If he himself had been wounded, he wore eagles' feathers colored red (*peji miknaka okolakiciye.*) Members of this society also wore necklaces and earrings, and the scalps that had been taken were worn on the arm in the dance. When these men prepared for a dance, they painted their whole bodies, usually a yellow color.

If one of them had stolen horses from the enemy, he showed the prints of hoofs on his legs. If he had saved a man from being killed by the enemy, he made the mark of a cross on his body or legs. When he had been wounded by a bullet, he represented bullet holes with drops of blood coming out of them. If a man had been terribly wounded, he put the red paint on thick around his mouth and chin, to show that the blood had poured from his mouth. The way in which their enemies had been killed, whether by an arrow, gun, club, spear, or knife, was clearly depicted on

the chests of the horses which were ridden into the dance.
Sometimes all those who had been wounded danced
together and sang a special song:

SONG
My friend has fallen
He has fallen in battle!

ODOWAN KIN
Mitakoda kdirpa yedo
Heciya kdirpa yedo!

The men who had captured prisoners and brought them
home were painted with a mark that represented a black
hand over the mouth. They danced by themselves and also
had a special song.

SONG
Friends, I let these prisoners walk
I let them walk in front of me
But I do not treat them roughly
I just let them walk ahead of me

ODOWAN
Koda, wayaka dena mani
Wicawakiya
Mitokam mani wicawakiya
Śicaya wicawakuwa śni yedo
Ikceya mitokam mani wicawakiya

The members of the Grass Society were chosen as were
members of the other societies. At the place of meeting,
when the time had come for the yearly election of officers,

Grass Dance. Nebraska State Historical Society, no. A547: 2-250.

two men were asked to bring them forward, and sang the following song:

SONG

Spotted Eagle,
You are a man
While you were living
You acted as though
You were a ghost

ODOWAN KIN

Wanbdi kdeśka wica yedo.
Niyaon qon he ehan
Wanagi wan iyecedya
Yaun wedo

Spotted Eagle, the son of Red Leaf, was a well-known man among the Dakotas. The term "acting as though he were a ghost" meant that he was bold and brave and did many daring things.

At the annual meeting the seven principal men of the Grass Society were supposed to tell any brave deeds that they had done during the year and then to hand over the articles belonging to their office. Five of them had belts made of crows' feathers, one a drum, and one a stick about eighteen inches in length trimmed with porcupine quills. There were as well a doorkeeper and a crier. When a feast was held, all the officers were fed by the man with the stick. With a stick he picked up the meat and other food and put it in their mouths, signifying that being so fed they should not fall into any bad habit. Every one of them was supposed to have killed one or more men. On returning from a raid, the brave washed himself and for several days was fed with the official stick on food taken from the enemy. If, however, upon his return he slandered his neighbors or committed other offences or omitted to bathe or to feed himself as prescribed for the allotted period, then, it was believed, he would never be able to rid himself of the bad habit of evil speaking or any other wrongdoing.

The members of this society subjected themselves to various acts of self-denial. Any sign of weakness on the part of a man whose wife had left him, such as following her and inducing her to return to him, was punished by dismissal from the society. He had failed to do the difficult thing.

Members of the Crow Society, *Kangi Yuha Okolakiciye*, wore the skins of crows with all the feathers as necklaces. Two of the seven principal men had warbonnets. These resembled caps or hats without brims covered with long crows' feathers. Two horns stood up on either side, decorated with beads and porcupine quills. Standing between the horns and covering the top of the hat were tufts or bunches of horsehair taken from the mane or tail and dyed a bright red. Such warbonnets were very showy affairs. Two of the members had lances, which were trimmed throughout their entire length with crows' feathers. Two others had whips, and one, a drum—all decorated in the same manner. The doorkeeper and the crier carried nothing peculiar to their respective offices.

This society was conducted in the same way as the others, the new members being collected and brought to the place of meeting and four or six women helping with the singing. The song had no words.

When all were assembled, the older men instructed the new members. One of the men held his warbonnet aloft and told how he had tried to live up to all that it represented; what he had done in war, the number of men he had killed, and in what way he had killed them. At this point, his sister or cousin burst into a song, the burden of which was equivalent to:

SONG
Saul has killed his thousands
David his tens of thousands

ODOWAN KIN
Saul koktopawinge kte
David koktopawinge kte wikcemna
Li, Li, Li, Li, Li, Li!
Li, Li, Li, Li, Li, Li!

The women sang praises of the noble deeds of the braves. After this the warbonnet was handed over to a new officer. If an owner of one of the warbonnets had been killed while fighting, he was represented by another man who told just how he had died, whether slain with spear, lance, arrow, or knife, and most important of all how he had made no out-cry in his agony. If possible, the warbonnet was always taken at once from the man who had been killed, so that it should not fall into the hands of the enemy, and was carefully brought back to camp.

The same forms were observed when the other princi-pal men handed over their lances, drum, and whips. The last were used heavily on the enemy in battle and were also applied to slow, lazy members in the Circle to encourage them to take part in the dance. The retiring officers talked a long time to those taking their places. Again we find the same advice given to a husband abandoned by his wife: "If that should happen to you, do not go after her. Leave her alone, and do not fight over her; she can never again be good. Do not whip your wife. A woman is weak, and if you whip her, you will be just like her. It is mean and low." (The speaker referred to the men in the tribe who did not belong to any of these societies—the very lowest class, who whipped their wives and did as they pleased.) "You must uphold the Circle; do everything for its honor within and be brave without in defending it from its enemies."

At the close of the meeting a dance always took place. Those who participated removed all their clothing except the crow-feather necklaces. Riding wildly into the dance, they leaped from their horses amidst a din of gunfire. Mounting again with reckless speed, they dashed away to some other point at which the same actions were repeated. Altogether, such a dance was a very wild and exciting affair.

Of the seven principal men in the Wolf Society (*Śunka Okolakiciye*), four had wolf skins, two had whips with the handles bound with wolf skin, and one had a drum. Those who received the skins wore them with a bunch of crow feathers fastened on just below the nape of the neck. The doorkeeper and the crier had no official objects. The members of this society traveled on foot, one man carrying the moccasins of the whole company in big bunches on each hip, while others carried the food in kettles. When they were about to go on the warpath, they all assembled in the middle of the circle and sang the following songs, addressing the first to the leader (whose name may have been, for example, Sitting Bear):

SONG

Sitting Bear, if you see anything
You must go close to it!

ODOWAN KIN

Mato Iyotanke, taku wandake cinhan
Kiyena da unwe!

SONG

Friends, look at me!
I am seeking as the wolf seeks!

ODOWAN KIN

Koda, wanmayake!
Śunke wakita qon miye yelo!

SONG

I do not want to pay any attention to girls
I must go and do my duty first!

ODOWAN KIN

Wioyuspapi kin wacin śni yedo
Tohantu keśa waku kte do epe do!

An incident—doubtless a rare one—is related of one
member of such a war party becoming fainthearted and actually leaving his comrades and returning to camp. The others
went forward, attacked the enemy, and brought back scalps
and horses. The following song greeted the deserter:

SONG (sarcastic)

I was going to (expected to) do those things
So I sent Weasel Eagle home to tell you about it

ODOWAN KIN (wiwicaknupi)

Ehanna decamon kta e,
Hintonkasan Wanbdi
Hośiku waśi qon!

Those who belonged to the Society of Warriors, *Zuya
Okoda-kiciye*, were very experienced in fighting and in hero-

ic deeds. Four of the leading men had shirts made of buckskin trimmed with porcupine quills; two had whips; and one,
a drum. The doorkeeper and crier had no distinctive objects.
At the yearly meeting, as in the other societies, the former
officers related what they had done. In case any one of them
had been killed during the year, the man representing him
narrated his story, took the shirt that had belonged to him,
and laid it carefully aside. It was the same in the case of a
man who owned one of the whips or the drum. They then
sang, as follows:

SONG

Hereafter, if the Society of Warriors
Should have a feast
And all the members are expected to be there,
Do not look for me!

ODOWAN KIN

Tohand Zuya Okodakiciye
Wicawotinna opapi
Owasin opapi nin econ ipi kta
Eśa amakitapi śni yo!

The new members had it impressed upon them that if
they did something inside the Circle that they should not
have done, they would be punished forever after death. If
they protected the Circle outside, by fighting, they would be
blessed forever.

It must not be supposed that in subjecting their sons to
the severe training and discipline described above, the Sioux
fathers were lacking in parental affection. On the contrary,
the fate of a young brave on the warpath was watched by his
father with the utmost solicitude. When bad news came and

a runner entered camp with the cry, "So-and-so's son lies down there," the stricken father was hard put to it to conceal his grief. The crisis had to be met with all the stoical calm available, but it was no less overwhelming. On such occasions the following touching lament was used, but even the lament was made a test of fortitude:

SONG

My son, you went off
For a little while
You are staying away too long!

ODOWAN KIN

Micinkśi, nankenunna
Idade ciqon, tuwa,
Dehanś unka!

This was supposed to be repeated four times. A father might get through the song once, but nearly everyone failed at the second attempt. After the fourth repetition the mourning one was allowed to weep, but to be overpowered by natural grief before the final repetition was considered weakness. The man who was able to reach the fourth time of singing praised his son's courage, as follows:

SONG

Yes, my son, you did well
You did your duty
You died fighting
You died without bringing disgrace on me
You died without bringing disgrace on your tribe

ODOWAN KIN
Ho, cinkś, tanyan ecanon
Hecanon kta iyececa
Kicizapi icunhan nit'e
Iśtedmayaye śni nit'e
Nitoyate iśtedwicayoye śni nit'e do

When the warriors left the circle, they were dressed and equipped for fighting. They were joined by members of the other groups who were ready to go out. Tipi Sapa described the excitement of seeing them gallop forth in their war paint and feathers with glittering weapons, many to be killed and wounded, others to return bringing home scalps and horses.

In all these societies, whoever first killed an enemy on the warpath secured the honors. Even if others who went afterward killed a great many more than the first, they received little credit. Everyone despised a society whose members had killed none of their enemies. It was said to them: "You have not done anything, you are disgraced!" Occasionally in times of peace there was a parade of all the societies. The braves who had died doing their duty were named, to an accompaniment of drums and the tuneless shout, "Li! Li! Li! Li! Li! Li!"

The horse plays a large part in the life of the Dakotas in festivities as well as warfare. The following occasion was remembered by Tipi Sapa. A certain man in the tribe who had been brought up in close contact with horses since he was a baby claimed that he knew everything about them. He held that, having lived with them so long, he was treated by them as one of themselves and had had their ways revealed to him. On one occasion he called the men who, in his opinion, had a thorough knowledge of horses to a meeting in a place outside of camp and addressed them as follows:

"Our tribe has secret powers. They have been imparted to me as leader of the horse dance, and they come directly from the Great Spirit. I will make songs for you to learn, and you must practice them hard. I should also like you to be prepared with some songs of your own."

The crier was told to go through camp and proclaim, "There will be a horse dance tomorrow, about noon!"

Those who were to take part in the dance were directed by the medicine man not only to paint their own bodies but to depict, on their horses, scenes representing exactly what had happened in the last fight. When they were in the act of attacking and killing, the enemy marks might resemble hailstones, for example, indicating that the last battle had been fought during a storm of hail.

When all was ready, the horse dancers put on their warbonnets and belts and provided themselves with shields, lances, spears, knives, whips, bows, arrows, and guns. After assembling, they were addressed by the leader, who told them that they would not be hurt because he possessed great power and knew they would be protected.

A great crowd of men, women, and children assembled for the occasion. At this affair, only young unmarried girls were asked to sing. They accompanied the drummers and together made up a kind of band concert. The horses were remarkably graceful in their movements as they stepped about and pranced and danced, keeping time to the music of the songs and the beating of the drums. The noise, excitement, and wildness grew fast and furious as the riders fired off their guns, shouted, and sped their arrows while the horses danced.

Sometimes during a short intermission the crier went about shouting, "This is all done for your amusement. You must give a smoke of your tobacco or something else to these people after all their trouble." The moment the music ceased, the horses all stopped dancing and of themselves turned directly around and faced the band. This was most remarkable, for many of them, though they had heard the drums in battle, had never before been in the dance.

During the next intermission, a great feast was held. Handsome presents of warbonnets, horses, and buffalo robes were given to the horsemen and to the young women who had helped with the singing. Then the wild dance began again and kept up all night or until the supply of songs was exhausted. That put an end to the festivities. After the people had left for their homes, the horse dancers went back to the central place from which they started. The leading man who conducted the meeting said:

> You see this man (meaning the head of the horse dancers) is very skillful in the dance and no bad accident has happened. He is the man to go to if we want this again. If there had been an accident, we would never ask this man who managed it to do it a second time. We will have only the one who knows the horses' ways. He is very kind to them. No matter how wild they are, they obey him directly and do whatever he wants them to do. He must be well paid for all the skill and power he has shown and the trouble he has taken.

Thus the horse dancers adjourned for a much-needed rest, the leader no doubt richer in reputation as well as in more tangible rewards.

War Stories

One type of warfare with its own special requirements was the stealing of horses at night. The party of men who had set out to steal horses halted at some point a safe distance from the enemy's camp. They gathered small sticks, one for each man, sharpened them, and stuck them in the ground at an angle— / / / /. After the men had returned from their dangerous errand, they learned who was missing from their number by the arrangement of these little pieces of wood. A stick pointing toward camp indicated that the man it represented had gone home. A stick broken in two and crossed showed that a man had been killed. If a stick remained as it was first placed, it served as a sign that its owner had not yet returned and was very likely either dead or badly wounded.

Another and more important mode of fighting consisted of regular and sometimes prolonged warfare between bands of men mounted on horses. The most courageous braves were chosen to take part in such conflicts. It was the custom, before fighting, to send out spies in order to learn exactly how the enemy was situated. These men always went out in the daytime. If one of them had seen the enemy and wished to let his people know, he did not take the time to return to them. He climbed the nearest hill, stood on the summit, and kicked backward. That meant, "The enemy is there, get ready for him!" Or he took off his blanket and waved it at them. This signified that there would be a fight at once.

War parties were often out at night. As they came back to camp, one of them gave a call or a prolonged yell. It was similar to the howling of a wolf, with two short barks at the end. The men in camp answered, "All right, you belong to us." Occasionally, someone came along and howled without adding the two short barks. This proved to those in camp that it was an enemy.

The best warrior among the Yankton Sioux, and a prophet as well, was a man named Red Leaf. He was very handsome—yellow haired and nearly six and a half feet in height. His people were on the verge of war with the neighboring Pawnees. The chief and leaders held a council to decide what was best to be done.

At this meeting Red Leaf was called upon to speak, and he talked a long time. He warned the people about a particularly dangerous warrior. "There is a man among our enemies, the Pawnees, that we have to look out for," Red Leaf said. "He has one white eye and is also left-handed. His nature is something like that of a wild cat—fierce, sly, and cruel."

Next day, when the Sioux rode into the fight, they kept in mind what Red Leaf had said to them. They determined to watch for this dreaded Pawnee and make him their target. A Sioux named Running Amidst, acting according to his name, rushed ahead and made a furious attack upon the enemy. He tried to hit the Pawnee and all the others around him, but in vain, owing to the uncontrollable restiveness of his horse.

Finally, Running Amidst managed to turn the beast around and attack the enemy, taking aim right and left, until he reached the Pawnee with the white eye. This man forthwith drew an arrow and shot Running Amidst through the body. The latter rode on with the arrow sticking in him. Upon seeing his comrades gather about him he said, "Friends, do all you can to them. They have now killed me." Shortly after that he fell to the ground. The Sioux jumped from their horses and rushed savagely on foot upon the Pawnees.

The left-handed man was fighting so desperately that no one dared to go close to him. Finally a little Sioux named Brazo came along and rode directly up to him. The Pawnee immediately took aim at Brazo. The latter made an effort to protect himself, holding his arm tightly against his body and face, but to no avail. The arrow of the white-eyed man went directly through Brazo's arm and penetrated his left side. Brazo then fought the Pawnee with fury. He struck him with his bow over and over again violently and so rapidly that he did not give him the slightest chance to pull arrows from his quiver. Upon seeing the situation, Brazo's friends gathered around and soon put an end to the dreaded Pawnee. The left-handed man with the white eye had, however, managed to do a good deal of harm, as foretold by Red Leaf, in killing one of the bravest warriors among the Sioux and badly wounding another.

His enemies secured the necklace of the Pawnee and brought it back to camp. The necklace was made of white corn with some blue grains here and there, and a bundle of medicines was attached to it. As the men were passing the necklace from one to the other and examining it by the campfire, seven grains of corn fell to the ground. When Red Leaf saw what the braves were about, he said, "Why did you not leave the necklace on the dead man? It is bad luck that those grains have dropped off. It means that seven of our next war party will be killed."

The following spring a band of warriors went out on foot led by a young man who carried a bell on a stick. They were accompanied by Red Leaf part of the way. After marching for some distance, they came to a place that seemed favorable for camping overnight. After they were seated around the fire, they were startled by a strange noise. It was the leader's bell, ringing violently of itself. Red Leaf, who had just come to the fire, told his friends that this was a sign of danger. A number of the party were frightened and returned home at once. If a man started out with a war party and after a time wished to return home because his courage gave out, he was allowed to go, but was held in great contempt. All his companions barked like dogs at him. The barking was a curse. They wanted him to feel that he was disgraced. If he left the party on account of being ill, he was not barked at, but permitted to depart in peace.

A man named Walking Crane said that he would not go back for any reason whatever; that he had come out to fight and that he fully expected either to be killed or wounded. This brave man, with twenty-two others, set out the next day to fight the whole band of Pawnees. As they drew near the timber of the enemy, they saw two women carrying wood into camp. One of the Sioux, Short-Haired Bear, said to Walking Crane, "Let us go and kill those women—they are enemies."

Walking Crane replied, "I fight only men. Kill them if you wish. You are just like them."

Short-Haired Bear and a man named Little Soldier ran toward the enemy's camp, the latter arriving first. They killed the two women and then went back to their party.

By this time the Sioux were surrounded by the whole band of Pawnees. Walking Crane thought it best to fight in the open, away from the timber. He placed men at intervals along the river. These twenty-three Sioux fought the enemy a whole day until they were overtaken by darkness. Then the chiefs of the Pawnees came forward and stopped the fighting.

Seven of the Sioux were killed, as Red Leaf had predicted, and eleven were injured. Only five remained uninjured. Little Soldier had his heel nearly shot off. His horse was shot and he hobbled a long way on foot. Finally he could go no further and lay down by the roadside.

Red Leaf, who had returned long before, and the other Sioux in "the home camp" saw a big crow with white on its throat and heard it say as it flew overhead, "Seven of your men have been killed. The others will be back by tomorrow night." Next day the war party came home, as the crow had said. They were hungry and had no clothes. The spring nights in their country were intensely cold, too. They told the people in camp that they had left Little Soldier behind. He was terribly wounded in the feet and had nearly lost his heel. His relatives, supposing that by this time he must surely be dead, wept, cut themselves with knives, and put on mourning. About four months afterwards, Little Soldier came home, a perfect skeleton. His experiences are narrated in the next chapter.

One time a party of Yanktons started out to fight but, as they drew near the enemy's country, they became very fearful. They could not rid themselves of the thought that they might all be killed. Having found a good place for camp, they shot two buffalo cows, roasted the sweet, tender meat and made a splendid feast. In the midst of making merry over their food, the warriors discovered that their horses had taken fright at something and had run away. This piece of ill luck was most alarming. They felt that they might be attacked at any moment and were quite unprepared to meet the enemy.

Next morning, they resolved to ask help from Little Brave, one of their number who was believed to have some knowledge of the spirits. He said he did not want to interfere

with the man who was with them, Walking Crane, who
knew all about the spirits and "secret things," but since they
had consulted him, he would try to do what he could. On
hearing this, they at once dug a grave, wrapped the wise man
in a buffalo robe as though he were dead, and let him down
into the ground.

While he was there, Little Brave called the spirits
about him and talked with them. After a time he came out
of the grave and spoke to the people, who were anxiously
waiting for him:

> You know we had a feast last night and gave
> nothing to the spirits. They are much offended
> with us because we neglected them, and it was they
> who drove our horses off to that lake we passed.
> The fine, black horse has broken one of his forelegs
> at the ankle. Our people will find them soon and
> bring them back. Perhaps you remember that a cer-
> tain man with us who knew some secrets (had hid-
> den power) told you that you would get some horses.
> The spirits that were just now talking with me said,
> "You and your people will soon have thirty-six head
> of horses, including two black mules; also, a man
> wearing a long red coat and carrying a bow, arrows,
> and revolver will be killed."

The party went without delay into the enemy's country.
They soon saw a man who wore a long red coat and carried a
bow, arrows, and revolver driving to pasture a herd of horses
including two black mules. As he belonged to the enemy, they
killed him, jumped on the horses, and rode away.

The following story about the role of calling forth spirits as part of warfare was told by Joshua Low Dog. Sitting

Bull's people, the Uncpapas [Hunkpapas], started out on one occasion to fight the Crow Indians. The latter came upon them un-expectedly, chased them, and killed twelve of their number. When this news was brought to the Uncpapas by the rest of the party, the whole tribe went into mourning. They felt that something must be done at once.

They visited one of their prophets and asked him to find out where the Crow Indians were. While the prophet called upon the spirits, the Uncpapas all seated themselves on the ground with bowed heads. Holding their pipes by the bowls with the stems pointing straight outward, they begged the "sacred ones" or "gifted men" to help the prophet.

After this, the prophet sang a song to the spirit:

THEY SING A PRAYER
When I call to the above
I sing for a Spirit
I sing for him to come to me!

ODOWAN WAN AHIYAYAPI
Wankatakiya hoyewaya can
Nagi kspa e wakidowan ye
Wakidowan cohan tiyata hi!

The other men turned their pipes around and smoked. The prophet told them where the Crow Indians were and just how many of them would be killed.

A party that included the prophet and was led by Low Dog, himself one of the "sacred men," went forward mounted on horses. They attacked and fought the Crow Indians, killing twenty-five of them.

Communicating with the Spirits

The Indians had various ways of communicating with the spirits in order to obtain their help in sickness or in fighting and in hunting. The men in the Circle who were supposed to know "secret things" were chosen for this purpose. The *pejuta wicaśa* (medicine man) was called for all kinds of diseases of mind, body, and spirit. He would bring his drum, made by stretching a dry hide over a wooden plinth, and his medicine ball. [When the buffalo were no longer plentiful, this ball was made of cowskin.] The ball was fastened to a wooden handle and inside it were pebbles. As the medicine man beat the drum with it, the rattling pebbles helped to frighten away the spirit of disease. The *pejuta wicaśa* would smoke his pipe of kinnikinick, offering the first smoke to the spirits. He would pray for their help and would sing and dance. He would use roots and herbs in some cases, but [the healing was] dependent upon the spirits, good or evil.

Tipi Sapa was well acquainted with a Yankton Dakota Indian named Crazy Walker. When the latter was about twenty-four years old, he announced that he was a buffalo man and had "the spirit of the buffalo." He went into the Circle carrying a buffalo hide with the skin tanned. Asking two young girls to help him, he gave a wooden basin with some water in it to one of them, and to the other, a pipe. The water in the bowl signified that the buffalo got strength from water; the pipe, as we have seen, was always used in praying to the Spirit, just as a young man, when dragging a buffalo's head, would turned toward it every little while with the pipe and pray for help.

Crazy Walker called four young men to him, one of them having a gun, another a bow and arrows. He asked them what they would like to have most, saying he had the power to give them anything they wanted. They all said that they wished to get married. Having put on his buffalo hide, he went over to a plot of soft ground some distance beyond his tipi and made buffalo tracks in the soft earth so that the people could see them plainly. He then got down on his hands and knees and cried out to the man with the gun or the one with the bow and arrows—whichever he happened to see first—to shoot him at once.

The youth obeyed and shot him directly through the body. The blood flowing out made Crazy Walker at first seem weak and faint, but after a while he got up and walked away. Many people did not believe he had been shot through and through, but he told them to come to examine him after he reached his tipi. Then he took some dirt or mud from the ground, rubbed it into the wound and healed it. Having "the spirit of the buffalo," he was now able to grant any requests. He asked the four young men if they had obtained what they wanted. They answered: "Yes, we have seen the girls we should like to marry." Crazy Walker said, "Will you keep them until they die?" and made them promise faithfully to do it. [This event occurred around 1860 and the last one of these women died in 1913.]

One time a band of Yanktons started out to hunt buffalo, but went a long way and found none. The wind, too, was

Making ceremonial arrows. Nebraska State Historical Society, no. A547: 2-241.

unfavorable. It was from the south and blowing behind them
instead of toward them; only a north wind is favorable for
hunting buffalo. They resolved to select a man to call up a
spirit to help them out of their difficulty. A young man
named Little Brave was chosen. He was bedecked with paint
and feathers and had a drum tied to one arm and rattles on
the other. Over his head and face was the skin or bag that
covers the heart of a buffalo.

He ran hither and thither, crying out and singing. All
the dogs of the band rushed out and barked at him but were
afraid to come near him. He told the people that the wind
would turn to the north by night and that there would be
two herds of buffalo very near them. What Little Brave predicted proved to be true. The next day brought them two
herds of buffalo, right at hand, and no end of fine hunting.

On another occasion, when the people had nothing to
eat and no prospect of anything, they called on a man named
Little Wooden Dish, requesting him to help them. He sang
and prayed [to communicate with the buffalo spirit].

Afterward he told the people that the buffalo would
come with a big blizzard and that after the storm was over
they would be thick all around the camp. The storm hit and
the people waited patiently for it to end. When it was over,
they looked about and saw buffalo crowding around so thick-
ly that they could shoot them from their tipis!

The following is the story of an Assiniboine medicine
man who used a special method of attracting buffalo. He
gave a certain kind of medicine to a young man who was a
good runner and said to him, "Go out and stand on that hill,
and rub some of this medicine on your arms and body. There
is a herd of buffalo near the hill and they will see you and
come forward. As they advance toward you, run and do not
let them overtake you. If you do, we shall lose them. When

you can run fast no longer, hide. Another man must be on the spot to begin where you leave off. Then he must have someone stationed at the point where he leaves off, and so on all along the line." The young man did as he was instructed; the herd followed each runner and was brought into camp, a distance of about four miles.

As we have seen, each band of Dakotas had men with these remarkable powers, which seemed like some sort of providence. Such men were always held in great honor.

*   *   *   *

When no buffalo were to be found anywhere, the fact remained that the people had to eat. A certain young man who seemed to have wonderful power was said to possess "the spirit of the deer" as others did "the spirit of the buffalo." He was chosen to call the deer to him. He selected a high, level piece of ground. He ordered a corral to be built at one end. Heaps of earth were placed at intervals along two lines that formed the letter V, the point being at the corral. Along each of these heaps of earth were willow sticks sharpened at either end and bent so that both ends stuck into the ground.

The young man, after painting himself in different colors, wrapped his buffalo hide around him with the fur outside and stood at the place he had selected. He held a pipe in his hand and pointed it toward heaven, to the four corners of the winds, and to the earth. Then he yelled out four times and sang, over and over again:

"See, those deer are coming now!"

Sure enough, a whole herd of deer came galloping by and went straight down the avenue of willow branches into the corral. Another herd followed and another until the entire corral was filled with the frightened animals. The people, who had been in hiding, rushed out and killed them with clubs. Tipi Sapa's father saw this done and declared it to be true.

Before the deer were skinned and the meat cut up and made ready for use, the young man told the people to take all the males and arrange them in rows by themselves and the females in rows by themselves. When this was done, they were to cut off the tip end of the tongue of each deer and give them all to him. If just one were overlooked, it would cause him to lose his power, so he went around and examined each animal with great care.

He kept the ends of the tongues, dried them, and made a powder of them. This powder he mixed with another medicine made of some kind of roots, then put it in a little bag and tied it in his headdress of feathers. The only occasion on which he wore the little bag was when he went out to call the deer.

Occasionally certain men were credited with a secret knowledge of what the enemy was doing outside of camp. These men tied flies' nests to their ears and shook them around as they danced. They were told by the flies of the movements and the plans of the enemy. Those who absorbed the power, or spirit, of the flies ranked with those who had the spirit of the buffalo or the deer.

FLY SONG
The things going on
Were told to me
By these black flies!

HONAGILA ODOWAN
Taku yukan hecinhan
Owasin omakiyakapi ece
Honagina sapena kin hena
Omakiyakapi ece!

Falling Hail, a medicine man, professed a special degree of knowledge regarding secret things. He dressed and acted at all times as though he were going to or were present at a ceremony of some kind. He traveled about the country dancing and telling of his doings but with the habit of always stating the opposite of what he meant. Falling Hail was tall, erect, and very fine looking. On one side of his head the hair was shaved; on the other side, it grew as long as nature allowed. Even in the bitterest weather he habitually took off all his clothes and painted himself, yet he never was known to take cold, nor was he ever frostbitten. He lived to a great age.

The habit of saying one thing and meaning another was also characteristic of Big Voice, a medicine man with whom Tipi Sapa was acquainted. He wore his hair very long on one side, and on the other he cut it off just above the shoulder. He had very handsome clothing and belongings. His shirt, blanket, and drum were beautifully trimmed with porcupine quillwork. This was done by his sister, who excelled in the art. Big Voice used to go into the circle, sing his secret songs, and dance. In summer, when he rode his horse down to the creek for a drink he generally sat on him backward. He often visited the girls, and if he fancied one, said to her: "I hate you! I don't want to marry you, so don't say yes!" The girl favored with his address usually knew enough to reply in the same manner, "No! I don't want to marry you!" Nevertheless, Big Voice had only one wife.

Tipi Sapa told of a time when Big Voice started off with a party to war. When the enemy's country was reached, he sent two men ahead to learn whether they were really at home. He found out that they were in the country and were preparing to make an attack the next morning. His men at once set to work painting their horses and dressing themselves. Meantime Big Voice had painted himself all over mud color and his horse the same but only on one side. He tied long strings of white linen to his bridle just below the chin. After these preparations he said to the people, "I am riding a horse of cloud. You see him. I have tied black cords to him (meaning the opposite of white linen strings). He will run all day." Next morning the attack was made. Big Voice reached the neighborhood of the enemy first and seized some horses. One of his men was killed and his scalp taken. As they were retreating, the enemy attacked them with great force, where-upon Big Voice shouted to his men, "Do not chase the enemy! Ride away from them!" He appears to have meant that they should turn around and give chase. He himself chased the enemy a long distance but never fired a shot because no one in his party ever told him not to shoot.

During the course of the fighting, he even pursued his own people and fired on them, making out that they were the enemy and that he was trying to defend his friends. He acted in this way all through the fight, until the enemy was worn out and the chase brought to an end. After it was over, the people said to one another, "Why didn't you tell Big Voice not to fire at the enemy? Then he would have done it and would have killed many of them."

This trick of saying and doing the opposite of what one meant seems not to have been unusual among the Dakotas. Whatever attraction it may have as a sport, it is hardly to be recommended as promoting either understanding or discipline.

[Miss Olden was mistaken in assuming that the "con-trary" behavior of certain men was merely a childish game played by adults. She did not understand the cultural/reli-gious context. Most of the so-called contrary behavior result-ed from strange requirements imposed on individuals by the Thunders in a dream or a vision. Basically the idea was that if the individuals were going to receive special powers, the spirits required them to set themselves apart from the rest of the people by engaging in strange behavior that was far enough from the norm to be noticed and to be a burden to the individual. The many instances where people failed to perform the activities demanded of them and consequently suffered crippling illnesses or even died were sufficient to convince the Sioux that even the most demeaning tasks required by the spirits should be rigorously fulfilled.]

*   *   *   *

[Miss Olden failed to include the following story of Red Leaf, the Yankton medicine man, in her book, although there is no doubt that Tipi Sapa related it to her. Tipi Sapa impressed upon his children the importance of Red Leaf, and the story of his spectacular feats was often told in our family. It was always told with such intensity and intimacy that I suspect Tipi Sapa had known Red Leaf quite well.

Red Leaf was orphaned at an early age, around eight or nine years old. He was taken in by his sister and her husband, but the man was terribly cruel to him and starved and beat him unmercifully. Red Leaf, distraught, ran away and soon found himself alone in a wilderness, completely lost and very hungry.

He gave up and threw himself on the ground, asking the Great Spirit to take his life. He lay on the ground a while. Finally he rolled over and looked up and saw an eagle nest at the top of a very tall pine tree. The eagle called to him, telling him life was precious and that he had much to do. Red Leaf sat up and stared at the eagle, skeptical and mistrusting. "If life is so precious, why is my life is so bad?" he asked.

The eagle said he would show Red Leaf how important life was by giving him gifts that he could use to help his people, because helping people was the most precious part of life.

Red Leaf was told to find a small, three-branched stick and make a small eagle's nest in it. Then he was to make a wooden bowl. The eagle showed him how to use these things to contact the spirits. Red Leaf learned a great deal from the eagle and thus encouraged, returned to his camp with his new gifts of the Spirit.

When he did a ceremony, Red Leaf would gather the old men in an oval formation. He would place the wooden bowl inside the oval. Then he would begin to sing the songs he learned from the eagle. He would dance around outside of the oval, taunting the men who were sitting with their backs to him, looking into the center of the oval. In his hand Red Leaf carried the little three-branched twig, and he would tell the old men that he was about to step into their oval and that none would see him do it. He encouraged the men to keep their eyes open while he crossed the line. None of them seemed able to observe him crossing into the center of the oval, and my grandfather told people that try as he might, he could never keep his eyes focused while Red Leaf stepped into the oval.

Then Red Leaf would dance around inside the oval. There was barely room to walk because the area was filled with the legs and feet of the old men. But as the men observed him, Red Leaf seemed to have plenty of room to dance. He then began to sing another song, again quite taunting, telling them that they should now watch him get into his nest. After dancing around four times inside the oval, he would suddenly jam the three-pointed stick into the ground near the wooden bowl, which was filled with water.

Then he would change his dancing so that he was running, and running quite hard, toward the little stick with the miniature nest. After several runs toward it, he jumped into the nest, which quickly became a massive eagle's nest in a tall pine tree. The wooden bowl became a large pond of water, and as the old men looked, they saw Red Leaf's reflection in the pool. They looked skyward, and there he was, nearly one hundred feet above them in the eagle's nest. He could then look down into the pool and see the past, the future, and anywhere in the world in the present.

Red Leaf became very wealthy as his powers to predict events, to find buffalo or lost things, and his healing powers caused everyone to flock to him for assistance. Walking Crane, one of the most famous Yankton warriors in the first half of the nineteenth century, was a stalwart supporter of Red Leaf and used him quite frequently, even though Walking Crane had many spiritual powers himself.

Since my grandfather told my father and his sisters exactly how this ceremony was performed and admitted that neither he nor Saswe was ever able to see Red Leaf get in and out of the nest, I suspect that he was on reasonably close terms with this spiritual person when he was in his teenaged years.

Ella said that the family was very disappointed that Miss Olden did not include Red Leaf's story in the book.]

*   *   *   *

On a certain occasion in the year 1876, Tipi Sapa invited Little Soldier and six other men to his lodge. When they arrived they heard the following incidents related by Little Soldier. [Little Soldier had been left severely wounded, with his heel nearly shot off and scarcely able to walk, after the fight with the Pawnees recounted in the preceding chapter. His account of what occurred following the battle so impressed Tipi Sapa because of its spirituality that this story became a family favorite that was retold over the years by many family members.]

When his companions were about to leave him for dead, Little Soldier called to them, "Make me a little shelter by this stream, in the shade of the willows, and let me have some bullets and powder." They did as he asked, then went on their way. Little Soldier remained there about ten days. He had scarcely any clothing and no blanket to wrap around him those cold nights in the springtime. The only way he could keep warm was by rolling himself about. He had little to eat. Sand turtles and small birds were the only kind of food he could get in that area.

He was not far from the camp of the Pawnees and could plainly hear the music and the shouts of the dance. Every night when he lay down, he expected they would appear and put an end to him. One evening as he was sitting at the door of his shelter, he heard someone talking in a very loud voice. He recognized the voice of Walking Crane, one of the seven men who had been killed in the last fight. Walking Crane said, "I thought they had all gone home, but here is one of them (meaning Little Soldier). We will go along with him."

Suddenly the seven men who had been killed all appeared and came inside the shelter with Little Soldier. The pipe was lighted, handed around, and smoked. Then they started out with Little Soldier and traveled the rest of the night. But as soon as day began to dawn in the east, the seven men gradually disappeared, simply fading away with the light. Little Soldier said to himself, "Well, I never thought these people had been killed. They seemed so real." But when daylight came, and they all grew dim and vanished away, he said, "Oh, yes, now I remember they were killed."

These same men appeared again the next night and took Little Soldier a long distance with them. At the first streak of dawn they passed out of view once more, leaving him alone. This went on for some time, until one night

Walking Crane said to him, "Tomorrow, in the daylight, you will see some hills with a growth of sagebrush at the foot of them. Coming out of the brush will be a deer; just fire at him and kill him." The next day, after the ghosts had left him, Little Soldier found the things exactly as Walking Crane's spirit said. He killed the deer, opened him, took out the liver and kidneys, and ate them. Then he peeled off the skin and thus provided himself with a warm covering.

Little Soldier remained in this place about thirty days. Then the spirits came back and asked him to go along with them again. Finally, after all this traveling, he found he had reached a place where there were fresh tracks of animals and people. He was evidently near the Sioux camp, but could hardly believe it. He dragged himself along for a little way but soon grew tired and sank down just outside the Circle. Some men who were walking by saw him lying there, and said to him, "Are you Little Soldier?" He said, "Yes." The men hurried back and told the people. They brought a blanket, placed Little Soldier in it, and carried it by the four corners into camp. His heel was quite well again but he looked and seemed like a ghost.

A story is told of a Yankton Sioux named Ash, who was taken ill and died. His body was neatly dressed in his best clothing and placed in the cemetery in a tipi on high poles, according to the custom. Everything was carefully arranged and the little door of the tipi was securely fastened.

The people in camp were about to move their quarters because they needed better pasture for their horses. The wife and the mother-in-law wished to see Ash before they left, so one night they went to the burying ground.

The mother-in-law became very tired and fell asleep. The wife sat for a long time crying bitterly. After a while, she thought she heard someone breathing heavily. She opened the door of the tipi and found Ash turned over on his side. He motioned to her to give him some water from a cup that was hanging on a pole. She handed it to him at once but saw that he did not drink well. His face was badly swollen as in death. Then the wife awakened the mother-in-law and hastened back to camp with her to tell the people.

On hearing the news, some of them went quickly to the cemetery, bringing a bed on poles swung over a horse. They put Ash on the bed and took him toward the camp. He refused to go into the Circle. He said he could not stand the smell of the people and wished to be kept out of the way of the wind that blew over from them. They took him to a place some little distance away, and the people went to see him there. After a while the swelling went down and he became more natural. Ash finally consented to go into the circle. He was led to the middle tent and questioned by the leading men.

One of them took up the pipe and pointed it to heaven, to the four corners of the winds, and to the earth. "Ash," he said, "we want you to tell us all that you can of the spirit world. God is your witness that you will tell nothing but the truth about what you saw." He agreed to do this and smoked the pipe with them.

He related, first of all, that he had walked along a path and had seen a man and his wife and a girl in front of him. He tried to overtake them, but could not, and lost sight of them altogether. He thought he was walking on the earth, but soon discovered that he was mistaken. He had reached a great height and on looking down saw the earth far below him; the path that was visible led upward. He came to the bank of a river and perceived the footprints of the same three people in the bed of the river. He could not tell whether he himself had walked through it or not. When he reached the other shore, he noted the traces of three people, from the water sprinkled on the sand. They may have been the same ones, but he did not know.

A great crowd was gathered on the other side. In a tipi he saw his brother-in-law, sister, and father. His sister brought something out and put it in a kettle over the fire to cook. As it boiled, it emitted a dreadful smell. At that moment his brother-in-law threw something toward him, a lasso made of buffalo hairs. He called out and said that he wanted Ash to give him his best horse. Ash replied that he would send him his fine bay horse and then went on his way.

He met some people who told him about an island that he was passing. He watched beings on it who cried and sang all the time about death. They were murderers, undergoing the horrors of everlasting punishment. He listened to the distressing sounds, then went on and on, a very long distance. Finally, he came to the tipi in the burying ground. He saw a man in it lying on his back and recognized himself. His ears burst open with a wh-wh-wh-sh. His wife was standing by his side trying to make him drink some water. Then he remembered that he was placed on a horse and carried to camp and that he refused to go into the Circle on account of the odor and until the swelling was down. Finally, there he was among them.

When Ash had finished his story, he told the leading men that he received the lasso made of buffalo hairs and wanted to secure his best horse for his brother-in-law. Just then, all the horses belonging to camp took fright and ran away from the water they had been drinking. Ash's fine bay horse, which he had promised as a gift, fell and broke his neck. So the spirit of this animal went to his brother-in-law in the far-off world.

Sun Dance. Nebraska State Historical Society, no. A547: 2-108.

The Sun Dance and Vision Quest

The annual Sun Dance of the Sioux was an occasion of great importance and significance. At the appointed season, runners were sent out to notify the different bands that they were all to assemble for at least two months during the summer. The latter part of June was a favorite time, for then the Juneberries were ripe and provided a welcome addition to the food supply. When the bands gathered for such an occasion, a very large circle was made, and in the center of it a great tent was erected. This tipi was occupied day and night by the leading men. Here they sat and talked back and forth, reviewing all that had been taught them and gaining fresh ideas from going over the old teachings. Upon their return to their respective bands they took with them whatever new learning or experience they had acquired in the conclave.

On pleasant summer evenings the young men put on their finest trappings and rode their horses all around the big circle. They made as much show as possible in order to attract the attention of the girls. Both girls and young men from the different bands would dress gaily, assemble in the circle, and dance nearly all night.

Toward the end of the purely social festivities, one of the leaders issued a solemn call to prayer. On hearing this, parties of young men rode off at once to the timber and gathered leaves from which to weave warbonnets. Leafy branches were torn from the trees and brought to the camp, where they were rapidly put together in the form of a booth or shelter near the large tipi in the center of the Circle.

Other young men cut the tallest tree they could find for a pole and carried it along swinging between horses. In the middle of the booth they dug a deep hole in which was placed a woman's workbag containing needles, scissors, beads, and porcupine quills, together with some buffalo fat. The pole was then set up and the hole filled in. From the top of the pole was hung a cross made of green leaves, to which was tied another workbag. These two bags signified liberty and freedom for the women at this special time. In fact, the pole thus erected in the early morning was properly called a "liberty pole."

The men painted themselves with the colors of the earth—red, green, yellow, brown, and black. They placed strings of otter skins around their necks and decorations of eagles' feathers over their chests. Skirts like those of the women were donned, while across their shoulders were thrown buffalo robes with the hair side out. On this great religious occasion, it was considered irreverent to touch any part of one's flesh with the fingers. In case it became necessary to touch the skin, little sticks neatly decorated with porcupine quills and placed in the hair at the top of the braid were provided for this purpose.

Thus prepared for the great ceremonial, a procession began to move toward the booth. It was led by a man carrying a buffalo head in front of the chief dancer, who carried the pipe. As they walked, the people mourned and wept. Passing into the booth they hung the buffalo head over the liberty pole. The pipe was laid on sticks provided for it and was used in the same solemn manner as it was on other occasions. The men sat in the booth in their buffalo robes while the singers arranged themselves about a dried buffalo hide stretched on the ground, upon which they pounded vigorously. The first tune was repeated four times, and all sang to the beating of the drum and the blowing of the flutes. When the chief singer threw off his buffalo robe and went out, the rest of the people did the same and followed him. It was then that the actual dance began.

A dancer gave a lasso, with a suitable gift, to another man selected to prepare him for the dance. The man was to draw up the loose skin on either side of the dancer's chest, on each shoulder, and frequently on the outside of each arm near the shoulder, and then pierce the skin and through the incisions draw the lasso and fasten it securely to the liberty pole.

After this the man danced furiously and pulled until his skin was broken. Sometimes, instead of the lasso, four buffalo heads were attached to the slits in the skin, two in front and two behind; the rapid motion of the dance caused the skin to tear. Every time a break was made in his skin, the relatives of the dancer had to give something to the poor. When all the skin was torn through, the women gathered around him and sang, "Li! Li! Li! Li! Li! Li! Li!" meaning, "What a brave man you are!" This great ceremony lasted two days and a night. During that time, not a morsel of food was touched, nor was anything taken to drink. After the sun went down, the dancers gazed upon the moon. It was the most sacred and solemn occasion of the year.

All the people followed the chief dancer, keeping step to the music, in the direction of the sun, which by this time was well up in the sky. They had many petitions to make and offered prayers through the sun to the Supreme Being. One man wanted horses and had tied small figures of them to his hand. Another desired to kill someone and carried a little image of his enemy. He sang the following:

SONG
Great Spirit, have mercy upon me!
Give him (my enemy) to me
With his horse!

ODOWAN KIN
Wakantanka onśimada ye!
Taśunke koya maqu yeyo!

After gazing steadily for hours in the direction of the sun, the man who wanted horses perceived a horse's head, so his prayer was answered. The one who desired to kill his enemy had the vision of a figure of a man appear before him, and he sang to avow the response to his prayers.

SONG
The Gros Ventre Indian said
He was going to come to me!
He is here now in spirit

ODOWAN KIN
Eca Rewaktokta he
U kta keye ciqon!
Wana hi yedo

Someone who prayed that he wished to be married had his prayer answered by seeing the vision of a woman. The Yankton men had a little song of their own:

SONG
You women,
keep away from me!
I don't want you!
I want a woman from
"The Burning Thighs"!

ODOWAN KIN
Winyan kin akoka
Econpiye yo!
Cicinpi śni yedo
Sicangu winyan ecena
Wacin ye!

The Burning Thighs (*Sicangu*) were the Rosebud Indians. If any of the Rosebud men wished to marry, they sang:

SONG
Go away (you woman!)
I do not want you!
I want to marry a
Yankton woman!

ODOWAN KIN
(Winyan) kin ako econpi ye!
Cicinpi śni yedo!
Ihankton wan winyan e
Bduza wacin yedo!

If a woman had been living with her husband according to the first or second form of marriage and had run away with another man, they sang:

SONG

Tall woman, why do you
Leave your home?
Your home is here without you!

ODOWAN KIN

Winyan hanska toka e
Tiwahe duha he?
Nita wakeya qon enna hedo!

Meaning: "You were respected. Why did you act in such a way? You have disgraced the tribe."

White Swan [chief of the Yanktons] was terribly thirsty from dancing night and day. Some men brought water, drank it before him, and sang this song:

SONG

White Swan, do you want
Any water?
Here is some water
We are enjoying it

ODOWAN KIN

Magaska qon mini yacin he?
Dena mini e unkiye qu
Unyatkanhan pedo

White Swan kept on dancing and paid no attention to those who were testing his resolve.

THE VISION QUEST

The most important and difficult step in a boy's life was that of learning to fast. For this purpose he was taken by his father to a high hill or butte, far away from his people. He carried with him, tied in a large sheet, an offering of food and various other things for the Great Spirit. The sheet was spread upon the ground on top of the hill, with its four corners toward the four points from which the wind came, and the offering was presented. The boy was obliged to remain in this place without food or drink for two days and two nights, and sometimes twice as long. He might become so weary that he would lie down a few moments upon the sagebrush. But he was supposed to stand all the time and to call without ceasing upon the Great Spirit to help him.

During such a prolonged fast he was likely to see a vision. Something having the appearance of a man would stand before him and tell him when he would receive help. This vision itself would always remain somewhere within reach, and it gave him his own song. No matter where he happened to be, if he were in any trouble he was to sing the song the vision had given and help would come. Here is an example of a vision song:

SONG OF THE VISION

I came here to you first
I came because you are calling me
I came from the Nation of Crows (East Wind)

I came here to you first
I came because you are calling me
I came from the Nation of Iron (South Wind)

I came here to you first
I came because you are calling me
I came from the Nation of Rocks (West Wind)

I came here to you first
I came because you are calling me
I came from the Nation of Wolf (North Wind)

WOMANYAKE ODOWAN KIN

Miye tokaheya wahiye
Miye co kin on wahiye
Kangi oyate e miye tokaheya wahi
Hinyapata wahi

Miye tokaheya wahiye
Miye co kin on wahiye
Itokaga maza oyate e
Miye tokaheya wahiye

Miye tokaheya wahiye
Miye co kin on wahiye
Wiyorpeyata tunkan oyate e
Miye tokaheya wahiye

Miye tokaheya wahiye
Miye co kin on wahiye
Waziyata šunka oyate e
Miye tokaheya wahiye

The vision advised him in this fashion: If you should
find yourself among any of these nations and in need of
help, sing these songs. You will be told what will happen.

Crows, iron men, rocks or stones, or wolves will be your friends in each place.

The vision would then disappear with a loud noise. The lad was filled with thankfulness for this encouraging sight. He called to the Great Spirit and told him he had seen a vision and that the future was as clear as the day.

Having to do his vision quest in a solitary place far from his people put the boy in much danger of being surrounded by enemies and killed. A story is told among the Sioux Nation of one of these young people who was fasting on a mountain, praying and crying aloud to the Great Spirit. Someone from his tribe happened to be wandering about in that neighborhood and heard him say as he prayed, "I see the enemy coming. I shall be attacked and killed." The man went home as quickly as possible and told his people. They gathered themselves together and hastened to the place where the young boy was. They found that the enemy was in fact approaching and there was a sharp fight before the boy could be reached. His people were victorious and saved his life.

It sometimes happened that the one who was fasting could not endure the strain and would run away. Possibly during the second night he would fancy that the hill or butte was shaking, but did not realize that it was himself. He thought that it would tumble to pieces and that he would be killed. Perhaps a terrible wind would come up. He imagined the full force of it was blowing directly upon him and was struck dumb with fear. He could stand it no longer but would run like lightning down the zigzag path and across the prairies. Worst of all would be the rattlesnakes crawling out of their holes and drawing nearer and nearer. He dreaded lest they should coil themselves around him and sting him to death. No power on earth or in heaven could induce him to stay a moment longer, and off he would go as fleet as a deer.

The boy who ran away would never have any power from the Great Spirit. He could not try the fast again so his opportunity was lost forever. He was also held in great contempt by his people. Some experienced man told the boys how difficult this "doing" was and exhorted them to be brave and never to run away. It very seldom happened.

[Charles Eastman remarked that the eastern Sioux—and he would have included the Yanktons in this designation—had much less brutal Sun Dance and Vision Quest rituals than did the Tetons. Tipi Sapa's versions of these ceremonies correspond to that interpretation.]

A Bundle of Tobacco –
Candi Woparte

During the winter of 1866, the United States government invited some of the Dakota chiefs and leaders to go to Washington. A number of them went and remained until the spring of 1867. The officials talked with these Indians about peace and tried to come to terms with them, but nothing of any importance resulted. On their return to Dakota Territory, François des Lauriers (Saswe), the father of Tipi Sapa, called a big meeting in camp on the Yankton Reservation. He suggested that bags of tobacco be sent to the different bands of Dakota with the request that they stop fighting with the white people. The Yankton Sioux acted on this advice.

In sending the message to another tribe, the Yanktons observed much ceremony in connection with the pipe and the bundle of tobacco. A buffalo-skin bag was filled with tobacco and kinnickinnick, fastened securely at the top, and painted blue. Several long pieces of the tobacco plant and a pipe were tied together in this bag and placed in a handsome cloth to be carried by the messenger. A man experienced in this "doing" took the pipe and went through the usual ceremony with it, saying to the Supreme Being, "Will you help us do this?"

He then explained to those assembled with him that the bag was painted blue because that was the color of the sky. Turning to the messenger, he said, "You will want a day for your errand with a clear blue sky when Wakantanka has moved away all the clouds. Go to these people and find a man who will listen to you." The runner set out for the camp of the other tribe and upon his arrival asked for the leading men. After the usual formalities, he laid his bundle before them and said, "I am sent here to ask you to keep the peace with the white people. You may suffer great injury if you persist in fighting with them. We Yankton Dakotas want to give you fair warning and we advise you to be friendly to the whites."

The leaders of the other tribe talked over the message and after weighing the matter well, either gave or withheld their consent. If a favorable answer was decided upon, the pipe was taken from the bundle brought by the runner. The usual oath was taken and the tobacco was smoked, thus binding the tribe to their agreement. On the whole, the Yankton Dakotas seem to have been honestly pacific toward the whites and to have used whatever influence they had with other tribes to bring about a friendly attitude. It is doubtful, however, whether their attitude was either recognized or appreciated.

The messengers were sent first to the Uncpapas, Sitting Bull's people, but met with no favor. The runners, shaking the dust of this tribe from their feet, passed on to the Minnekanwojus (Planting near the Water). Having left their own reservation, these people were then living in Montana along the Powder River.

When the messengers came into camp, the leaders who were assembled around the campfire asked them whence they came. The runners answered, "We come from the Yankton band." "What do you want?" asked the leader of the Minnekanwojus. "We want you to stop fighting the whites," replied the messenger of the Yanktons, "and come back to your own reservation and settle down."

After much discussion, the chiefs and leaders finally agreed to do as the Yankton leaders suggested. Taking the pipe and pointing it to heaven, to the four corners of the winds, and to the earth, they filled it with tobacco from the bundles of the Yanktons, smoked it, and made their solemn oath to the Supreme Being above. So the pledge was made. Then turning to the messengers, they said, "Go back to your own chiefs, my friends, and tell them this: 'You are kind; you are thoughtful; we accept your bundle of tobacco.'" The Minnekanwojus agreed to return to their reservation in the neighborhood of Fort Bennett, and as a pledge of good faith, agreed that their chief, White Swan, would come in the following spring as the representative of his tribe to renew with the Yanktons the oath to which his tribe had bound themselves.

On his arrival, White Swan was received most cordially by the Yankton chiefs and urged with great solemnity to remain faithful to the most solemn oath which it was possible for an Indian to take—the oath sworn over the pipe and the bundle of tobacco. Meantime Little Hawk, one of the leaders of the Uncpapas, had reconsidered the Yankton proposal and had decided to enter into an agreement with General Custer. (Edward, the son of Little Hawk, lived in Wakpala and was a communicant of St. Elizabeth's.) His plea was based on the ground that his people did not wish to fight with the whites, but did desire liberty to roam freely as heretofore and to hunt the buffalo without being disturbed.

Custer smoked the pipe with them, thereby taking the oath of peace. The leader of the Uncpapas then said to him: "If you break this oath, you will be punished by the Supreme Being; if we break it, so will we suffer." The conclave was a solemn one, the oath, at least in Indian eyes, the most binding possible. But Custer appears to have been unimpressed. The oath was broken almost immediately. For two months desultory fighting continued. Then came the battle of Little Bighorn and General Custer's death.

[This narrative combines a sequence of events into one story. The actual course of events described here unfolds over the period 1867–1875. The Great Peace Commission to the western tribes was authorized in 1867, so it is likely that the Yanktons who had been in Washington that previous winter were asked by the government to act as intermediaries for the commission. Thus, sending out the tobacco bundle was a logical development, since one of the major problems of the Peace Commission that year and in 1868 was to make certain that the "right" Sioux leaders were sworn to peace.

In 1865 the government had sent a treaty commission up the Missouri River to sign treaties with any group of Sioux that happened to meet with them. Returning to Washington with these treaties, the commission and the president were stunned to learn that the treaties did not end the war on the Bozeman Trail. The men who had signed the treaties did not possess the authority to do so. With this failure only two years before, it seems reasonable that to ensure the success of the Peace Commission, friendly tribes like the Yanktons would be enlisted in the effort to bring peace to the northern plains. Tipi Sapa was fourteen years old at the time the tobacco messengers were sent out, and he was therefore old enough to attend meetings with his father on matters of this gravity.

The Yankton plea for peace must have encouraged other Sioux groups to look more favorably on the efforts of the Peace Commission in 1868 when the big Fort Laramie treaty was signed. We then have a hiatus of approximately eight years, until 1875, when General Custer was stationed at Fort Abraham Lincoln after his expedition into the Black

Family on reservation, ca. 1900, Nebraska State Historical Society, no. A547: 1-4.

Hills in 1874. While at Fort Lincoln, Custer encouraged the northern Sioux to make formal peace treaties with the tribes at Fort Berthold, and in May and June of that year the people of Cheyenne River and Standing Rock did sign treaties with the Arickaras. At least one of these treaties was in written form and has survived to this day.

Almost certainly Custer would have had to smoke the pipe with the Sioux people at these two agencies and with the people at Fort Berthold to get them to consider making peace with each other. It must have been during this time that Custer promised not to harass the Hunkpapas and Blackfeet, as recounted by Edward Hawk. While this story has a parallel with the Cheyennes smoking a pipe with Custer, also after the Washita massacre, it seems likely that this story was also true.

Tipi Sapa was particularly proud of his association with peace efforts before he became a Christian, since it confirmed for him the idea that his life's mission was one of bringing peace and harmony to the Sioux people. During the prolonged period when the Yanktons were negotiating for compensation for the Pipestone Quarry in Minnesota, the old chiefs, led by Struck-by-the-Ree, told their lawyers that the Yanktons were custodians of the quarry on behalf of the whole Sioux Nation. They said that one reason why they sent out bundles of tobacco and pleaded with the other Sioux tribes to make peace was that they had obligations to try and make peace when the whole nation was at war with another nation. Whether this was true or not, I cannot say, but it is certain that all the other Sioux tribes recognized the Yankton ownership of the quarry. Even the Sissetons, who had gotten an article in a treaty suggesting that they had an ownership claim, quickly backed away from their stance when confronted by the Yanktons in 1858.]

Afterword

The original account in *The People of Tipi Sapa* did not focus on one group—the Yanktons, the Standing Rock people, or the Sioux people who followed Tipi Sapa in converting to Christianity. Each of these groups could properly be said to be Tipi Sapa's people. Miss Olden apparently mixed together the stories Tipi Sapa told, some of which were from the Yanktons, others from the people at Standing Rock. The original text also split some stories into two parts and put them in different chapters. She continually expressed disbelief in some of the accounts of spiritual experiences, which must have irritated my grandfather no end. I have had to add explanations and rearrange much of the material to present a proper reading of what Tipi Sapa told her.

After Tipi Sapa the stories of these people for the most part are sad and illustrate what happens to the small communities of unique people inside a gigantic industrial society. The Yanktons lost considerable land in the period 1910–1920, when the allotments of many of the people were taken out of trust by the government on the excuse that they had proven themselves competent to live in white society. The Indian clergy in particular had their lands put into fee simple, and they soon lost them to taxes. The business committee of the Yanktons seems to have become inactive after they succeeded in receiving compensation for the loss of the Pipestone Quarry in the mid-1920s. With the coming of the New Deal, hardly any land remained in tribal hands. The people resisted the Indian Reorganization Act of 1934, which affirmed the right to self-government but under a structure and bound by rules determined by the U.S. government. The Yanktons demanded in congressional hearings that the Act be repealed with respect to their reservation in the early 1940s.

After World War II, the U.S. Army Corps of Engineers began a massive public works program that had a devastating effect on the Yankton Reservation. The Pick-Sloan project built a series of large earthen dams on the Missouri River to generate electric power, flooding most of the good bottom land owned by the Yanktons. The little settlement at White Swan Landing was completely flooded, and the graves were removed to cemeteries in Lake Andes. My father and aunts lost several allotments they had inherited in this area, and many Indian farmers were wiped out. The payments they received for the loss of their bottomland were hardly sufficient to purchase comparable land away from the dam. The little town of Greenwood, where most of the mission work began, became isolated. It was no longer the center of social, political, and religious activities, so many of the people moved away.

Since the traditional council of band leaders had always dealt with outside threats and relied on kinship customs to regulate their domestic affairs, many Yanktons came to believe that they had never had a government. With the coming of the New Frontier, the tribe began to reorganize itself, but decades of inactivity had convinced scholars, lawyers, and even tribal members that their tribal government was a novelty created for the purpose of receiving funds in the War on Poverty. With the onset of legalized gambling, the tribe finally secured an income-producing industry and began to provide services for its members.

Standing Rock did not escape the invasion of the industrial world either. In 1912 the government forced allotment on the people, and thereafter the loss of land doomed the small villages on the reservation. Wakpala, where St. Elizabeth's School was located, declined dramatically from an important cattle-shipping terminal on the railroad to a small village without industry or population. The old business section virtually vanished, leaving only a church and a brick schoolhouse.

The reservation organized a more formal government under the Indian Reorganization Act (IRA), but it was never clear whether the tribe had formally accepted the law. Standing Rock was host to many of the Black Hills Treaty Council meetings that succeeded in getting legislation to allow the Sioux into the Court of Claims to press for compensation for the loss of the Black Hills. Although the case was dismissed in the early 1940s, it was revived in the late 1950s and finally settled in 1980. The Sioux tribes rejected the settlement, and although Congress appropriated the funds and deposited them in the U.S. Treasury, no Sioux tribe accepted the money and jointly they pushed for a different resolution to this problem.

What damage the allotment didn't do to Wakpala, the Pick-Sloan project finished. Oak Creek, which ran along the valley just south of St. Elizabeth's, was flooded for a considerable distance, destroying all the cottonwoods and other trees and eliminating the bushes and shrubs that used to provide the people with foods and medicines. Since the water level of the dams was adjusted periodically, Oak Creek became a mud flat that bred mosquitoes in the summer and provided no firewood in the winter. Standing Rock did get some compensation for loss of plants and bushes, but it was hardly sufficient to enable the people to live as they once had. In recent years the tribe has successfully negotiated additional payment for the use of tribal water in the Missouri for the purpose of generating power in the Oahe dam.

The church work, as previously noted, declined steadily throughout the twentieth century. With the refusal of the mainstream Protestant missionary churches to recruit and ordain Native clergy, the most promising young people began to look to careers in the federal government or local school districts as areas in which they could succeed. With the recognition of IRA governments, secular functions quickly took precedence over religious commitments. Indian congregations were now served by inexperienced non-Indians who stayed a few years and then sought greener pastures. The Kipling-inspired romance of mission work—taking up the white man's burden—died in the 1930s, and with diminishing financial support from the national church, the mission schools that had served the Episcopalian Sioux began to be phased out, to the distress of the people. Bishop Hare School at Mission, South Dakota, was closed, then revived briefly as a boarding home for Indian boys, to allow them to attend the local Todd County public high school. St. Elizabeth's became a boarding home and eventually was turned over to the tribe for the social programs it was operating. Finally, in the 1980s St. Mary's School at Springfield, South Dakota, was closed.

At the height of their influence, the mainstream denominations had created many chapels on the Sioux reservations, with some chiefs demanding their own church building and guild hall before they would allow their people to join a church. Social programs of the Depression, followed by World War II, dislocated many Sioux people to locations outside the reservations where they could find employment. Most of them never returned to the reservations. Many of them would return to their home chapels for the special holidays such as Christmas, Easter, and Memorial Day, but attendance during the rest of the year at these chapels was minimal. People simply did not live in small enclaves anymore. School consolidation on the reservations meant the decline of many of the "camps" where people continued to live in the old tióšpaye way.

The Niobrara Convocation, which had helped the Sioux continue their old gathering at mid-summer, flourished for about a decade after World War II, as many reservation people had acquired automobiles and could therefore travel to this statewide gathering. By the mid-1950s the powwows and emerging Sun Dances directly competed with the convocation, and people increasingly identified Niobrara with white culture and the powwows with their own culture. People also did not camp as had their parents. Nearby motels provided comfort and enabled delegates to go back and forth to the church meetings, so that attendance at many functions began to shrink significantly. It was considerably more difficult to gather people informally in motels than it had been to stroll around a large camp circle of tents as in the old days.

The Sioux people, like my grandfather, had embraced the hymns rather than the doctrines of Christianity. Some of these hymns when sung in Dakota fit the tune better than the English words. Much of the activity at the Niobrara Convocation was simply people gathering around the church organ in the evenings and singing the hymns for hours. But English was becoming the language of the people now, and so even this cherished activity began to fade.

The people at church headquarters in New York City began to use Niobrara as a fund-raising gimmick. Beginning in the late 1950s, the convocation saw an increasing number of eastern visitors who had to be honored for merely attending the gathering. Where Niobrara once had three or four thousand Indian people in attendance, by the 1980s a big crowd was numbered in the hundreds. As many people sat in deck chairs observing the services as were in attendance at the services.

There is no question that Christianity served as a bridge to enable the Sioux people to make the transition from their life of freedom to a new life confined within the small boundaries of a reservation. In spite of modern popular political doctrines, there should be little doubt that many Sioux embraced Christianity when their traditional social institutions and the practice of their own religion were prohibited to them. The men's and women's societies of the old days continued as part of the new religious life of the people. Meetings featured traditional oratory as people debated the programs for their societies for the coming year.

Kinship responsibilities did not falter as people accepted the new religion. The better families followed most of the old ways and kept track of their relatives, although with intermarriage with non-Indians and people from other tribes, kinship also began to falter and accommodations had to be made.

It should be clear from the Black Elk literature and other works, and from my grandfather's discontent in his later life, that Christianity did not replace the old Sioux beliefs and practices. The core of the traditional religious ways continued to provide a foundation upon which another religious tradition could be seen to be useful for a short time. Thus the current interest in traditional Sioux ways is not in any way a contradiction.

Index